NATIVE AMERICAN TRIBALISM

Indian Survivals and Renewals

D'ARCY McNICKLE

Published for
The Institute of Race Relations, London
by
OXFORD UNIVERSITY PRESS
New York   1973   London

Ornament appearing on Chapter opening pages: Apache rawhide shield with cover, 1860-1880. Photograph courtesy of Museum of the American Indian, New York, Heye Foundation.

The maps that appear on pages 16, 17 and 18 are reproduced by permission from the *Annals* Map Supplement #16 of the Association of American Geographers, Volume 62, 1972.

PREFACE

The forceful occupation by a band of angry Indians of the Washington, D.C., headquarters of the Bureau of Indian Affairs in November 1972, and the seizure three months later of the village of Wounded Knee, South Dakota, again by protesting Indians, grew with a certain logic out of the events described briefly in these pages. They occurred too late to be included in the body of this account and it seemed important to relate them to what had gone before.

Until these recent years, whatever happened to the original inhabitants of native America was determined in far places, by people of a different history and tradition. Because the native Americans lacked a system of writing, because they considered land to be a common resource open to all who could make use of it, and because they governed themselves without bureaucratic structures they were deemed incompetent to share in building a new society. That society, in fact, found no place for them except as wards of the state.

At different times and by various men in places of power

the harsh reality of conquest was tempered, to the extent of recognizing their ownership of the soil and their right to govern themselves in internal matters. These rights were even stipulated by royal decree and supported by judicial opinion. The exercise of these rights was never free of interference and encroachment, however. Men who administered Indian affairs seemed always to have the uneasy feeling that no governing body could operate on a consensus basis and they were impatient with the delays often occasioned by the lack of consensus. Perhaps it also troubled them when tribal matters were discussed in a tribal language—how could the intricacies of government and modern technology be expressed in a *primitive* language! Administrators and bureau lawyers frequently stepped in to "correct" a tribal decision, to negate an action, or to dictate a procedure.

At the bottom of these misgivings and over-the-shoulder promptings was the certainty that native America had vanished before the march of progress and that individuals and communities had no business trying to perpetuate the aboriginal past. Indians had no future as Indians. The congresses of the mid-1950s accepted the judgment without questioning it.

This certainty had already manifested itself in the closing years of the last century, when Congress authorized the individualizing of tribal land holdings as a device for detribalizing the people. By dismantling tribal structures, it was asserted, nothing would stand in the way of transforming Indian communities into standard American communities. This led finally to the effort of the mid-twentieth century to legislate Indians out of existence by destroying the guarantees that had protected their remaining lands and their tenuous hold on self-government.

The anger that exploded in Washington and at Wounded Knee had its kindling point in the acts of the Eighty-third Congress (1953-54), by which two major tribes and several lesser Indian communities were destroyed. The first reaction among tribal groups was dismay and disbelief. Then they were caught up in fear, as they wondered which of them would be the next victims. A trait commonly shared by native Americans is to draw back from danger, not to challenge but to wait and watch. In this instance, when the first shock had passed and younger Indians began to speak out, to demonstrate, and to join protest movements, their elders turned upon them and charged them with acting in un-Indian ways. This did not deter the young activists, many of whom were veterans of World War II and the Korean War, and many had college training. Their experience in the larger society taught them that passive acceptance would not win respect for their people, and they were determined to earn respect.

What followed, further bewildering the elder traditional tribesmen, was the creation all across the country, and in Canada, of action-centered organizations voicing protests or advocating policy reforms, and accompanying these organization efforts was a proliferation of local and national mimeographed and printed news sheets. The white man's weapon, the written word, was being wielded by the native Americans with enthusiasm, if not always with quality printing.

A further discovery followed. Having taken the protest course, the young militants found that results are not immediate and in the best of circumstances what is gained is not always what was sought. As a consequence of a series of conferences and congressional hearings conducted during the 1960s, sweeping policy changes were recommended in education, health care, employment opportunity, resource development—in all the areas in which the Indian people were disadvantaged—yet reservation living conditions remained unchanged. Infant mortality rates were excessive, life expectancy was short, housing was deplorable, unemployment rates ran nine and ten times higher than the national rate.

The response was intensified protest. Alcatraz Island in San Francisco Bay was occupied in November 1969. Sioux Indians camped on top of Mount Rushmore, where the faces of four United States Presidents are carved on a granite cliff, to demand the return of the Black Hills, the sacred mountains of the Sioux people. The Pit River Indians in northern California seized property of the Pacific Gas and Electric Company which, the Indians insisted, had been wrongfully taken from them. In the Canadian province of Alberta, Indian parents kept their children out of school to dramatize their opposition to the government policy of enforced integration. In the Pacific Northwest, Indians defied state authority by conducting "fish-ins" in defense of treaty-guaranteed fishing rights. Demonstrations such as these erupted in epidemic numbers across North America.

Briefly in the summer of 1970 hopes were raised by President Nixon's message to Congress giving strong verbal support to the principle of Indian self-determination and proposing the statutory creation of a Trust Council Authority to safeguard Indian interests in land and water. He also proposed that the Bureau initiate a program of contracting with Indian tribes for the performance of administrative and management services provided by the Bureau.

After more than a year, nothing had happened. In fact, every effort by a team of young Indians brought into the Bureau to translate the President's message into program activities was effectively nullified by old-line employees, some of them Indian, who evidently resented being supplanted by the young activists. The frustration of those months prompted an incident which foreshadowed what would come later. The incident was a physical skirmish in the Washington headquarters building of the Bureau in September 1971, when riot police were called to the scene to arrest protesting Indians. No damage occurred, other than wounded feelings, but the Indians learned that officials charged with administering Indian affairs were difficult to approach for the purpose of presenting a grievance.

These embittering experiences, sharpened by the brutal handling, including murder, of Indians in South Dakota and California, climaxed in Washington, D.C., in November 1972. What started out as a peaceful but determined effort to petition the government, involving caravans of Indians traveling from all quarters of the country, was met by temporizing public officials who misjudged the temper of the petitioners. The outcome was the seizure of a government building and its forceful occupation. Incidental to the occupation extensive property damage occurred and irreplaceable records destroyed or carried away.

The Trail of Broken Treaties, as the movement was called, was sponsored by eight national Indian organizations. Representatives of these groups, meeting in advance of the journey to Washington, adopted a 20-point position paper which could have been the basis of peaceful negotiation. Of the twenty points, seven were concerned with the restoration of the treaty relationship disestablished in 1871 and with other aspects of treaty review, implementation, and enforcement. These requests were at first ignored, and only after open violence erupted were the Indians given assurance that their position paper would be formally received and acted upon.

One outcome of the Washington episode was the dismissal of several ranking officials, including the Commissioner of Indian Affairs, Louis R. Bruce, and the Associate Commissioner, John O. Crow, both Indians, who had been at odds for some time. The Bureau ceased to operate for a time and faced the prospect of a major reorganization. An unfortunate outcome was a deep division within the Indian community between those who favored militant action and therefore supported the Trail of Broken Treaties, and those who favored the older Indian way of talking in council. They were distressed by the destruction of official records, since these had to do with land and water and other issues affecting the economic future of reservation life.

The confrontation at Wounded Knee, South Dakota, between opposing factions of Indians as well as between Indians and established authority served further to divide the Indian people at a time when unity seemed essential. Wounded Knee had a special significance for all Indians, but especially for the Sioux people, since it was on Wounded Knee Creek on a frigid December 29, 1890, that soldiers of the 7th Cavalry, General Custer's humiliated troop, slaughtered almost three hundred men, women, and children coming to surrender.

The trouble at Wounded Knee brought out in the open a conflict that the Pine Ridge Sioux tribe had been caught up in for almost forty years. A written constitution adopted by the tribe in 1935 under the authority of the Indian Reorganization Act provided for an elected tribal council representing reservation districts. Like other Plains tribes, the Sioux had no centralized government, but each of the major divisions of Sioux-speaking people was made up of local bands or camps organized around one or more leaders. Decisions were arrived at within the local group without outside interference. An elected council, such as the 1935 constitution established, displaced the camp structure and made no provision for traditional leadership. Most of the older leaders refused to vote in a tribal referendum adopting the constitution, and in general they abstained from voting in elections for tribal representatives. Such refusals were intended to express disapproval, but the effect was to place control of tribal affairs in the hands of members who were in part assimilated to the white political system, were often of mixed blood, and were not at home in the Sioux language.

The years since 1935 had been turbulent years at Pine Ridge. Tribal officials were frequently charged with misuse of funds, with favoritism toward relatives and callousness toward all others, and in general with acting in un-Indian ways. Just such a local embroilment was responsible for the explosion that turned the small community of Wounded Knee into an armed camp.

Impeachment proceedings had been lodged against the incumbent tribal chairman, and when the effort failed his opponents asked the American Indian Movement (AIM) for moral support. This national Indian organization had played a leading role in the Washington affair as well as in a number of other protest incidents. And now in South Dakota it was to appear in a contradictory role. Whereas before the leaders of AIM had campaigned against bureaucratic control over Indian lives and Indian property, now the same leaders called upon the bureaucracy to depose the Pine Ridge tribal chairman and to abolish the 1935 constitution. The Secretary of the Interior, upon whom this demand was made, had no authority to interfere in either instance, but if the authority had been his, and he had invoked it, the last vestige of a tribe's sovereign right to govern itself in internal matters would have vanished. While the federal government sent in arms and men and established a cordon to confine the occupiers of the community, and gun fire from both sides resulted in the deaths of two Indians and the wounding of a government official, the threat of force did not degenerate into the wanton use of force.

The besieged Indians agreed after several weeks to lay down their arms and evacuate the community, but when the time came to deliver their weapons only some few rusty shotguns and other weapons of doubtful effectiveness appeared. Those possessed of serviceable firearms had slipped away during the night, taking their weapons with them. It was an old Indian habit.

These incidents, born out of anger, brought into sharp focus attitudes and presumptions whose validity was no longer acceptable. Indians had not asked for the Indian Reorganization Act. The Pine Ridge Sioux had not asked for a written constitution and an elected council. Men of good will had assured them that these were good things to have, and the Sioux had tried to live with the assurance, though it divided their loyalties. At an earlier time men had decided that it was a good thing to individualize tribal community lands. And before that was the decision that it was a good thing to discontinue the practice of making treaties with Indian tribes. These were not decisions in which Indians shared, and in fact their capacity for decision deteriorated as men of presumptive good will acted for them. Older Indians had tried to live with that reality, seeing no way around it, hence their unwillingness to challenge the forces around them. If they waited and talked quietly among themselves, perhaps the forces would wither away and they would not have to surrender what was left.

So the anger of the young was in part directed at the old men of the tribes, but that was anger within the family. The real targets were the men in far places, of good faith or bad, who still thought of themselves as the only proper source of Indian well being.

It now seems likely, after Washington and Wounded Knee, that anger will hang in the air, like a combustible vapor, for some time to come. Indian Americans need assurance that riots are not essential preliminaries for purposeful talk.

Albuquerque, N.M.   D.McN.
June 1973

CONTENTS

NATIVE AMERICAN TRIBALISM

1 A GENERALIZED VIEW

The assumption had come down from earliest times, not always voiced, but implicit, that the native inhabitants of the New World would become extinct. They belonged to an inferior race and must give way to a stronger. As Count Alexis de Tocqueville was moved to remark in 1831 while he watched a muted body of displaced Choctaw tribesmen, "The Indians have been ruined by a competition which they had not the means of sustaining."

The notion grew stronger as the settlers waxed in numbers and the demand for living room accelerated. Reference to "the vanishing red man" became a common theme in song and story. James E. Fraser's equestrian statue, "The End of the Trail," first shown at the San Francisco Exposition in 1915, captured the note of inevitable doom. Reproductions in miniature of this doleful composition had wide distribution as parlor ornaments and carried into middle-class homes the idea that Indian destiny had run its course. If this occasioned regret, it was no more deeply felt than that expressed for the extermination of the passenger pigeon and the buffalo. Such losses were accepted as part of the cost of taming a wilderness world.

Only the Indians seemed unwilling to accept oblivion as an appropriate final act for their role in the New World drama. Caught up in succeeding waves of devastating epidemics and border wars as settlement moved westward, the Indians retreated, protecting what they could, and managing to be at hand to fight another day when necessity required it. They lost, but were never defeated.

That there had been spectacular losses is well documented by the woeful record of epidemics, one of the earliest of which struck the New England tribes in 1616 and left a clear coast for the Plymouth landing. An especially devastating smallpox epidemic in 1781-82 swept through tribes on the upper Missouri River and northward as far as Great Slave Lake, paralyzing the fur trade for two years. The Mandan tribe was virtually wiped out in 1837-38. The Pawnee tribe lost a fourth of its population in 1849. Indians of California were hunted like rabbits by boisterous gold miners, and the native population of that state was reduced from an estimated 100,000 in 1850 to less than 20,000 in 1906.[1]

By 1850 the total Indian population for the area covered by the United States was about 250,000 according to estimates that may not be accurate (the count may have been less), while for Canada in that year the figure, equally speculative, is given as 90,000. This is what remained of an aboriginal population of perhaps 850,000 for the United States and 220,000 for Canada.[2]

1. See Robert F. Heizer and Alan T. Almquist, *The Other Californians*, Berkeley: University of California Press, 1971, pp. 23-64, for a summary of atrocities committed against Indians during the years 1850-70.

2. For the Canadian Indian population, see M. C. Urquhart, and K. A. A. Buckley, *Historical Statistics of Canada*, Cambridge University Press, 1965, pp. A2-14. For the United States the material is summarized in J. Nixon Hadley, "The Demography of the American Indian," in *The Annals of the American Academy of Political and Social Science* (afterwards referred to as *The Annals*), vol. 311, May 1957, pp. 23-30.

Then the tide turned, slowly at first. Within the first two decades of the present century it was possible to question the assumption of ultimate extinction. The gains were not notable until about 1930, but in each decennial census since then the rate of growth of the Indian population in both the United States and Canada has exceeded the rate for the general population. As health facilities improve and become more readily available to the Indian people, the growth rate should continue to improve until, before the end of the present century, the Indian population north of Mexico will be what it was before Europeans came upon the scene. By the end of the seventh decade, the Indian population in the United States had climbed to 700,000 while in Canada, with 220,600 Indians reported in 1967, the lost ground had been regained.

The enumeration of Indians has always been beset by special problems, an understanding of which will provide some insight into the contemporary Indian situation.

It should be explained, for example, that in the United States Indians are not counted as Indians unless they fall within certain categories. Usually this means Indians for whom the federal government has some responsibility to provide services. The government prefers to limit rather than expand this number. Thus, many thousands of individuals are not counted, though they are as much Indian by inheritance and style of living as those who are officially enumerated. The reasons for this often have historical beginnings.

In the regions of earliest contact—the Atlantic seaboard and the states fronting on the Gulf of Mexico—tribal territories were appropriated and the indigenous population was either destroyed or driven inland. But in recent times from the swamps and coves and wooded mountains of those regions Indians appear in growing numbers, and it is apparent that extermination was never complete. They had disappeared from the scene and their tribal territory had been dissolved before the United States came into existence, and therefore no treaty relationship or other basis of recognition was established.

In the area north of the Ohio River and westward to Lake Michigan, a different course of events produced quite similar results. After the American Revolution, settlers poured into the region, using the Ohio River as a main highway. In the single year 1787, flatboats loading at Pittsburgh transported 18,000 men, women and children, 12,000 head of livestock, and 650 wagons to new homes along the reaches of the river. The struggling new government tried to pursue a policy of preventing settlement until treaties could be negotiated and the lands transferred in an orderly manner, but so great was the pressure for land that years of confusion and border warfare ensued. Eventually, the tribes in the area, with the exception of portions of the Iroquois nation, signed treaties of cession and moved westward.

But there were dissenters. Indian families, or bands, or parts of bands either chose to remain behind on land allotments, as the treaties often permitted, or simply refused to abide by the agreement and in effect cut themselves off from the main body of the tribe. These Indians still remain in the Great Lakes country, growing in numbers, but not officially recognized as Indians and therefore not enumerated.

In Canada, Indian status is even more arbitrarily determined. A person defined as an Indian under the British North America Act may not be an Indian, by reason of enfranchisement, under the Canadian Indian Act. This can lead to the anomalous designation "non-Indian Act Indian." The definition is further complicated by distinguishing between treaty and non-treaty Indians, and here historical accident is the determining factor. Some Indian groups never entered treaty relationships with the government simply because the government failed to negotiate, and therefore their status and their rights in the lands they occupy have never been confirmed. And finally a large population, consisting of persons of Indian ancestry who were not part of a recognized Indian social or political group and therefore were not eligible to negotiate a treaty, have no status at all as Indians. They are the half-breeds, or Metis, who usually live in distinct communities and whose biological makeup and lifestyle may be as Indian as the inhabitants of a neighboring treaty reserve.

The University of Chicago studied the problems of identifying and enumerating the Indian population, with results quite at variance with official reports. At a time when government programs in the United States and Canada still predicated Indian assimilation, the Chicago study concluded that "Indian communities, as separate, distinct social systems, are increasing in population." As to these communities, even where there had been a history of "long, intensive contact with Euro-American society, the common acculturation pattern is for these small societies to take over, possibly, a great many Euro-American traits and institutions, but to fit them into a context of the older covert Indian patterns of life. More than tentatively, one can say that American Indian communities, as a whole, are distinct growing communities that still preserve the core of their native style of life."[3]

The conclusions of this study carry the subject beyond the consideration of numbers alone as a measure of Indian survival. The evidence for this ongoing Indian world is diverse and pervasive. Of the estimated 300 Indian languages spoken in the area north of Mexico at the time of discovery, at least half are in current use. Great numbers of Indian children start their formal schooling without knowledge of the English language—and pose a problem for their English-speaking teachers.

Kinship systems and lines of descent still function, often at

3. Robert K. Thomas, "Population Trends in American Indian Communities," paper prepared for the American Indian Chicago Conference, June 1961.

variance with government record systems and legal procedures. Individual Indians who dress, speak, and act like any contemporary American or Canadian, still play prescribed roles as clansmen, as members or even as heads of ritualistic societies, and as upholders of an older social order.

It has recently been remarked that "Few Indian tribes have disappeared completely," and while this is a surprising fact to most white men, it "indicates that these people are not being absorbed or assimilated into the dominant American culture. Indeed, American Indian groups still retain many aspects of their distinctive ways of life and in only rare instances become Americanized."[4] The observation applies with equal force to the Indians of Canada.

Various explanations have been offered for the persistence of Indian communities and tribal identity. At an earlier time it was asserted quite simply that these original inhabitants were incapable of assimilating the culture of the dominant society. They remained Indian because they could not reach beyond what they were. This view was starkly stated during a debate in the United States Senate in 1871, when a Senator from Illinois declared, "The Indians cannot be civilized; they will not be civilized; they do not want to be civilized. . . . We must treat them as savages."[5]

The point of view contained an inherent contradiction, since those who professed it were often the same ones who advocated coercive measures requiring the "savage" society to adopt the habits and values of Western civilization.

A more rational modern thesis, put forward with some empirical findings, proposes a correlation between basic personality structure and cultural persistence. The best documented

4. Edward P. Dozier, George E. Simpson, and J. Milton Yinger, "The Integration of Americans of Indian Descent," *The Annals*, pp. 158-65.
5. *Congressional Globe*, 41st Congress, 3rd session, 1871.

studies in this area are those conducted by Professor A. Irving Hallowell and some of his students dealing with the Chippewa Indians—in Canada related bands are designated Ojibwa and Saulteaux.

These Indians occupied an extensive area north of Lake Huron and around both shores of Lake Superior westward to Lake Winnipeg. Contact with Europeans through the fur trade occurred at an early date and their modern descendants display a wide range of acculturation. The northern group along the Berens River in western Ontario follow a hunting-trapping-fishing economy very close to the aboriginal mode described by early travelers and traders; and at the southern extreme the Wisconsin Chippewas live in close contact with their white neighbors, speak English, send their children to school with white children, and dress and behave very much like the whites.

The purpose of the study was to determine, if possible, what agreement or conformity existed between observable acculturated behavior and the covert, inner life of the people. The general outlines of post-contact Chippewa culture were reconstructed from the accounts of explorers, traders, missionaries, and others who had close association with the Indians in the seventeenth and eighteenth centuries. This descriptive material was supplemented by field observations and projective tests administered to adults and children.

Hallowell had expected that the Wisconsin (Lac du Flambeau) Indians "would exhibit a radically different personality picture from that of the northern Ojibwa." But this proved not to be so. He reported that, contrary to expectation, the studies furnished "a considerable body of evidence that all points in the same direction—a persistent core of psychological characteristics sufficient to identify an Ojibwa personality constellation, aboriginal in origin, that is clearly discernible through all levels of acculturation yet studied. For this reason all the Ojibwa referred to are still Indians in a psychological sense, whatever clothes they wear, whatever their occupation, whether they speak English or not, and regardless of race mixture."[6]

Hallowell does not contend that continuity precludes change, but only that change occurs without obliterating the personality structure. Indians remain Indians not by refusing to accept change or to adapt to a changing environment, but by selecting out of available choices those alternatives that do not impose a substitute identity. In 1871 the Senator from Illinois in his diatribe was expressing an impatience, which others have voiced before and since, over the Indian trait of taking the white man's horse and gun and liquor without surrendering to the dominant society.

But to say that a culture persists or that a modal personality remains psychologically intact while adapting to change does not describe what it is that persists. It is necessary to define content or quality, at least in generalized terms, in order to determine what sets one culture apart from others, and possibly to distinguish stages within a sequential development. This is not easy because any culture is itself a generalization, an averaging out of many discrete modes, even contradictions. When the problem is dealt with quantitatively by cataloging the known traits of a culture, the result is an abstraction describing nothing human.

George and Louise Spindler suggest some characteristics of Indian personality that seem to have the quality of universality. Using the data of psycho-cultural studies, individual biographies, and direct observation, they describe certain widely shared psychological traits which, in their view, "characterize

---

6. A. Irving Hallowell, "Ojibwa Personality and Acculturation," in *Acculturation in the Americas*, Sol Tax, ed., Selected Papers of the XXIX International Congress of Americanists, vol. 2, p. 110, 1925. See also Hallowell's *Culture and Experience*, Philadelphia: University of Pennsylvania Press, 1955.

in a very general sense limited aspects of the aboriginal personalities of American Indians and possibly characterize the pan-
Indian psychological core of the least acculturated segments of
contemporary tribes."[7]

There can be disagreement in naming the elements that
should be included in such a psychological inventory, as the
Spindlers were aware when they suggested the following: re-
strained and non-demonstrative emotional bearings coupled
with a high degree of control over aggressive acts within the
group and a concern for the safety of the group; generosity
expressed in varying patterns of formalized giving or sharing;
autonomy of the individual in societies that were largely free
of classes or hierarchies; acceptance of pain, hardship, hunger,
and frustration without voicing complaint; high regard for
courage and bravery, often patterned as aggressive acts against
the out-group; fear of the world as a dangerous place, sometimes expressed as fear of witchcraft; joking relationships with
certain kinsmen as a device for relieving pressures within the
group; detailed, practical, and immediate concern in problem
situations, rather than advance planning to avoid difficulties;
dependence upon supernatural power, invoked through dreams
or ritual, as a means to the good life.

If the concept of the universal psychological trait is valid,
leaving aside the difficulty of agreement as to which traits have
that quality, it offers insight into the reasons for cultural persistence. To the extent that shared traits exist, they would determine, as through a perceptual screen, what the group accepts
and what it rejects among the choices made possible by a changing cultural environment. In any case, Indian characteristics
exist and remain in play after centuries of Indian-white association. The Dominican monks, who in 1544 described Indians as
"not acquisitive" and "satisfied with having enough to get along

7. George D. and Louise S. Spindler, "American Indian Personality
Types and Their Sociocultural Roots," in *The Annals*, pp. 147-57.

on from day to day," were describing traits that are complained of in modern times, by the aggressive, hustling white man.[8]

These views respecting the persistence of Indian culture and personality have not gone unchallenged. Some students working with the Chippewa-Ojibwa material, for example, question whether a viable native culture can be said to exist among a people whose way of life, in this case hunting and fishing, has been thoroughly dismantled, leaving them dependent on sources outside their communities. Personality formation, it is argued, is a cultural product and when a culture ceases to function it also ceases to determine human development. One critic of Hallowell's findings insists that "Modern circumstances . . . are more important in the lives of the modern Indian of Ojibwa ancestry than whatever Ojibwa cultural factors, subtle or not, may still survive," and concludes, "to the extent that Ojibwa personality traits can be said to persist, they persist as functions of modern situations."[9]

The trend in this later criticism is to view the Indian people as an exploited class within the general population, deprived of access to sources of power and to the labor market. In this view, the effort to define modern Indian personality in terms of aboriginal culture values is romantically beguiling but scientifically untenable.

The debate does not clarify the question, although it has called attention to the conditions of Indian life, some details of which will be examined further along.

As a matter of simple observation, Indian communities do exist, distinct from other American or Canadian communities, and while their resident populations fluctuate as individuals leave and return, their numbers continue to increase. These are

8. Lesley B. Simpson, *The Encomienda in New Spain: Forced Native Labor in the Spanish Colonies, 1492-1550*, Berkeley: University of California Press, 1929, p. 169.
9. Bernard J. James, "Continuity and Emergence in Indian Poverty Culture," *Current Anthropology*, vol. II, no. 4-5, Oct.-Dec. 1970, pp. 439-41.

communities of poverty for the most part, but they do not merge with the rural poor in the areas where they occur, and when individuals leave for urban centers and find themselves in urban ghettoes, they do not merge with the ghetto population. The social and economic forces that play upon the lives of the non-privileged lower classes affect Indian lives as well, but with a significant difference. As a minority group within the general society, Indians take their cues from their group; they do not regard themselves as deprived members of an affluent society and they do not feel impelled to acquire status in that society. They may seek greater economic security and proper recognition of their political rights, but they pursue these ends in order that their own societies may endure.

While these are the observable facts, the interpretation of the facts and the bearing they have upon the continuity of Indian culture allow for differences of view. A common assumption, one that endures with surprising hardiness, is that native cultures can only deteriorate under the impact of a stronger economic and political power; they cannot accommodate to change and still retain distinctive traits of their own. As a corollary, it would have to be argued that the only cultures that remain pristine and therefore viable are those that remain in hostile isolation from all outside cultural encounters.

What is remarkable about this view is that it takes no account of a common characteristic of the Indian people: they call themselves Indians, or more precisely, they refer to themselves by their own linguistic designation. This is the practice, however far removed the modern designee may be from his buffalo hunting or seed gathering ancestor.

Why this is so, why in spite of massive forces moving them away from the familiar past Indians can retain a sense of who they are, is probably best explained by the phenomenon of "ethnic boundaries" described by Frederik Barth. Pertinent here is his observation that "Culture contact and change . . .

is a very widespread process under present conditions as dependence on the products and institutions of industrial societies spreads in all parts of the world. The important thing to recognize is that a drastic reduction of cultural differences between ethnic groups does not correlate in any simple way with a reduction in the organizational relevance of ethnic identities, or a breakdown in boundary-maintaining processes."[10]

And elsewhere: "The nature of continuity of ethnic units is clear: it depends on the maintenance of a boundary. The cultural features that signal the boundary may change, and the cultural characteristics of the members may likewise be transformed, indeed, even the organizational form of the group may change—yet the fact of continuing dichotomization between members and outsiders allows us to specify the nature of continuity."[11]

While scholars dispute among themselves over the question of cultural survival, the people who are the subjects of the dispute continue to think of themselves as Indians, to act like Indians, and perhaps to puzzle over why their existence should cause so much confusion.

In more substantial ways Indians have survived into the present. Both in the United States and Canada they own and utilize land, timber, water, minerals, and other property—tag-ends of their aboriginal territory. Again, in the United States and in Canada, they occupy a special status within the law, a condition that is not always to their advantage but is a recognition of the sovereignty they once exercised as self-governing people.

The reserved land base, as we shall discover, like the population, went through a period of severe reduction. Most of the major Indian reservations, or reserves, as they are termed in Canada, were created before the end of the last century, usually

10. Federik Barth, *Ethnic Groups and Boundaries: The Social Organization of Culture Differences,* London: George Allen & Unwin, 1969, p. 32.
11. *Ibid.,* p. 14.

by treaty. In spite of many years of turmoil, of border fighting, and Indian defeats and removals, the tribes managed to stay within the general region of their aboriginal domain. The exception to this is the eastern United States, from which the Indians were removed by legislative fiat and armed force. (See maps, pages 17, 18, and 19) As late as 1890, the tribes in the United States retained a total area of 140 million acres, a land surface almost as large as the state of Texas, and this at a time when the total Indian population was at its lowest ebb and the idea of ultimate extinction was generally accepted.

Policies and legislative action pursued after that time resulted in the transfer of large acreages out of Indian ownership. Indian society itself came under heavy attack by a benevolent paternalism determined to accomplish the assimilation of the Indian people without delay. The methods and procedures instituted in pursuit of this objective were at times hostile, at times benignly wrongheaded, and always destructive.

Thus, the generalized picture today is of a people that has survived in numbers, in social organization, in custom and outlook, in retention of physical resources, and in its position before the law. The situation might be described as a survival of fragments, of incomplete entities—but there we would miss the mark. Any people at any time is a survival of fragments out of the past. The function of culture is always to reconstitute the fragments into an operational system. The Indians, for all that has been lost or rendered useless out of their ancient experience, remain a continuing ethnic and cultural enclave with a stake in the future.

Let us now examine in closer detail how these conditions and consequences came to be.

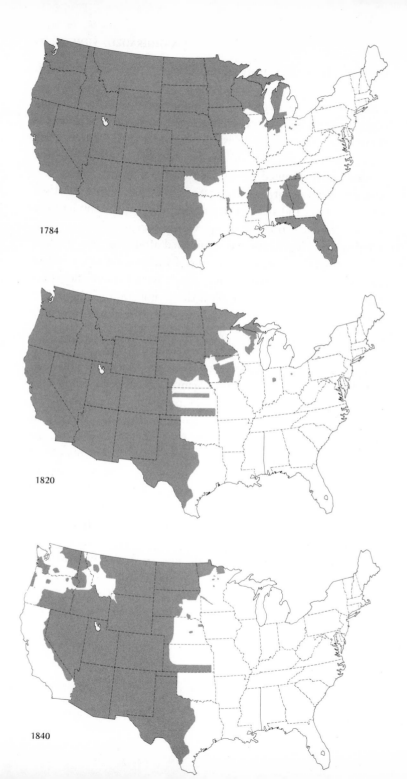

1784

1820

1840

INDIAN LAND CESSIONS

Ceded land
Unceded land

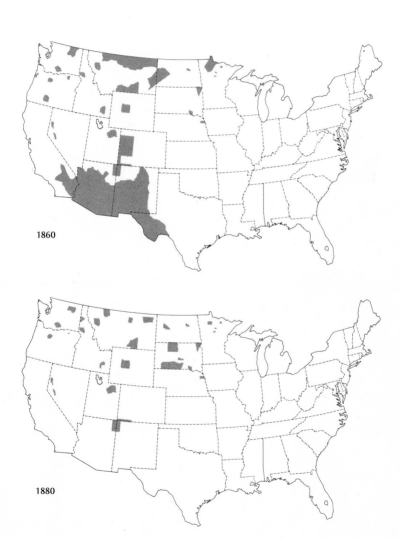

1860

1880

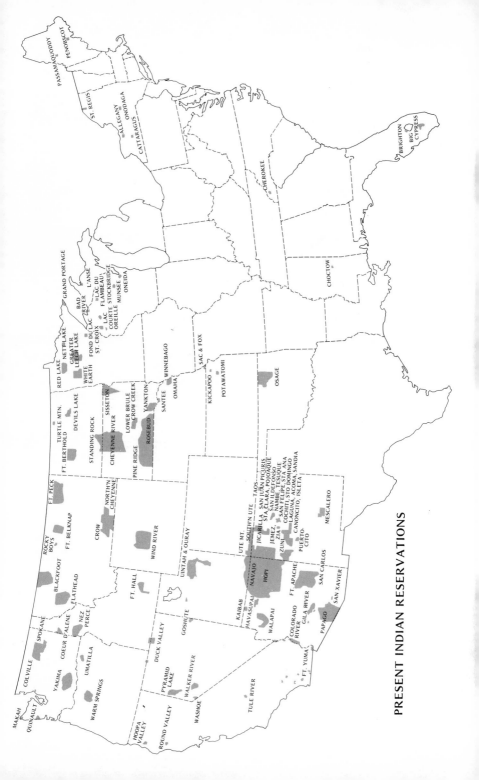

PRESENT INDIAN RESERVATIONS

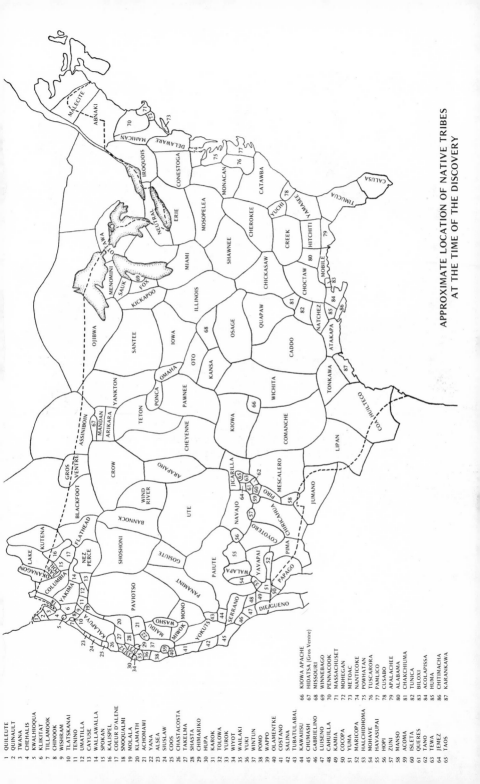

APPROXIMATE LOCATION OF NATIVE TRIBES
AT THE TIME OF THE DISCOVERY

1 QUILEUTE
2 QUINAULT
3 TWANA
4 CHEHALIS
5 KWALHIOQUA
6 KLIKITAT
7 TILLAMOOK
8 CHINOOK
9 WISHRAM
10 TLATSKANAI
11 TENINO
12 UMATILLA
13 CAYUSE
14 WALLAWALLA
15 SPOKAN
16 KALISPEL
17 COEUR D'ALENE
18 SNOQUALMI
19 MOLALA
20 KLAMATH
21 ACHOMAWI
22 YANA
23 ALSEA
24 SIUSLAW
25 COOS
26 CHASTACOSTA
27 TAKELMA
28 SHASTA
29 CHIMARIKO
30 HUPA
31 KAROK
32 TOLOWA
33 YUROK
34 WIYOT
35 WAILAKI
36 YUKI
37 WINTUN
38 POMO
39 WAPPO
40 OLAMENTKE
41 COSTANO
42 SALINA
43 TUBATULABAL
44 KAWAIISU
45 CHUMASH
46 GABRIELINO
47 LUISEÑO
48 CAHUILLA
49 KAMIA
50 COCOPA
51 YUMA
52 MARICOPA
53 HALCHIDHOMA
54 MOHAVE
55 HAVASUPAI
56 HOPI
57 ZUNI
58 MANSO
59 ACOMA
60 ISLETA
61 QUERES
62 TANO
63 TEWA
64 JEMEZ
65 TAOS
66 KIOWA APACHE
67 HIDATSA (Gros Ventre)
68 MISSOURI
69 WINNEBAGO
70 PENNACOOK
71 MASSACHUSET
72 MOHEGAN
73 NANTICOKE
74 POWHATAN
75 TUSCARORA
76 PAMLICO
77 CUSABO
78 APALACHEE
79 ALABAMA
80 CHAKCHIUMA
81 TUNICA
82 BILOXI
83 ACOLAPISSA
84 HUMA
85 CHITIMACHA
86 KARANKAWA
87

Karok woman basket weaver; she also wove her hat. *(Smithsonian Institution National Anthropological Archives, Bureau of American Ethnology Collection. Photographed by Gov. John Daggett, prior to 1902.)*

Modern basket weaver, Papago Reservation, Arizona.

Theodore B. Hetzel

The kayak, or skin-covered canoe, was designed several thousand years ago in the Bering Sea region, possibly by the Aleut people. *(Smithsonian Office of Anthropology. Photographed by Merle LaVoy, prior to 1925.)*

Taos Pueblo man fleshing deer hide for tanning.

Theodore B. Hetzel

Preparing tortillas, traditional breadstuff, Papago Reservation, southern Arizona.

Theodore B. Hetzel

Splitting salmon in preparation for drying. The woman in foreground is using the *ulu*, traditional woman's knife.

Theodore B. Hetzel

2 COLONIAL ANTECEDENTS

The European nations intruding themselves into the world of the Indians had two practical problems to solve. First, they must occupy the land and defend their occupations against the indigenous tribes and other European powers. In the second place, they found it prudent to devise procedures by which title to the land could pass in an orderly manner from Indians to Europeans.

The most direct solution of both problems would have been extermination of the natives, and in the first years of her New World adventure, Spain almost accomplished this in limited areas, but quite unintentionally. In their eagerness to exploit the riches of the new land, the first settlers captured whole villages of the peaceful Arawak and either shipped them back to Europe as slaves or set them to laboring in newly opened mines or on plantations. The Arawak—Columbus found them "a loving people, without covetousness," whose "speech is the sweetest and gentlest in the world"—retaliated by dying in droves or by disappearing into the mountains.[1] The native population of Haiti, which was the first center of Spanish activity, declined from an estimated 200,000 to 29,000 between 1492 and 1514.

This drastic reduction was recognized as undesirable; indeed, it occasioned the first reform program in Indian administration. The Laws of Burgos issued in 1512 were not of much help in saving Indian lives, but the enactment of an ineffective law is not unique in Indian experience. The Indians were saved by practical circumstances. If that initial trend had continued, the Spanish would have found themselves without a labor force and profitable enterprise would have suffered.

Extermination as a policy encountered other difficulties in those first years. Pope Alexander, in return for arbitrating the rival claims of Spain and Portugal in the New World, insisted that the peaceful conversion of the native inhabitants should have primary consideration. Policy and action were constantly brought up short by this injunction. In other instances, landfall occurred in regions where nature was inhospitable or where the Indians were not a "loving" people and offered such resistance that shore parties were thankful if they saved their skins.

Colonizing efforts in the north were especially hazardous and barely managed to survive the first years. Eccles describes Jacques Cartier's winter at Stadacona (Quebec) in 1541: "From mid-November until mid-April the fort and the ships were buried under several feet of snow and ice and sub-zero winds howled across the frozen river. As though that were not enough, the men were stricken with scurvy. By mid-February only ten of the crew of 110 were even moderately healthy."[2]

Of 108 colonists who landed at Jamestown in 1607, only sixty-two were alive six months later. The Massachusetts ex-

1. Paul L. Ford, ed., *Writings of Christopher Columbus*, New York, 1892, p. 165.
2. W. J. Eccles, *The Canadian Frontier: 1534-1760*, New York: Holt, Rinehart & Winston, 1969, p. 15.

perience was quite similar; "scarce fifty" out of the hundred who went ashore at Plymouth survived the first winter.

Spanish exploration and settlement was invariably an armed invasion and military posts were established as an incident of settlement. When rebellion was attempted, as in 1495 while Columbus was in Spain after his second voyage, retaliation was prompt. The Indians were subdued and several shiploads were transported to Spain and offered for sale by the Bishop of Burgos, who was also Minister in Charge of Indian Affairs. Thus in the very first years in the New World, Spain cut the pattern that she would follow with such devastating results for the Indian tribes in Mexico and Peru.

There was, however, a core of positive accomplishment in the colonial policies and practices of the Spanish regime. Spain was the first to give formal recognition to the occupancy rights of the Indians and to defer to tribal self-government. The Laws of the Indies, proclaimed in 1542, provided specifically on these points that "Indians are free persons and vassals of the crown . . . Lawsuits among the Indians are to be decided . . . according to their usage and custom . . . Nothing is to be taken from the Indians except in fair trade."[3]

These laws were a codification of earlier pronouncements and orders of court. They were an outgrowth of an opinion rendered in 1532 by Francisco de Vitoria, who boldly asserted that non-believers were not precluded from owning property and, therefore, the Indians were entitled to the ownership of their land and should be dealt with accordingly. He wrote, "The Spaniards have the right to go to the lands of the Indians, dwell there and carry on trade, so long as they do no harm, and they cannot be prevented by the Indians from doing so."

While Spanish policy changed from period to period and lax administration often defeated sound purpose, the effect of the Laws of the Indies was to bring the Indians under the pro-

3. Lesley B. Simpson, *The Encomienda in New Spain*, p. 169.

tection of the crown and to anticipate the practice of trusteeship incorporated into law by the United States and Canada and provided for by the United Nations with respect to dependent peoples.

A modern commentator offers this analysis: "During all of the Spanish regime the least protection given to the Indians was that governmental approval had to be obtained before any transfer of land from Indians to Spanish settlers was valid. . . . The Indians [occupied] a position before the law in one sense approximately equal to that of a native of Spain, and yet a more favorable position, because the Indian thereby became a special ward of the Crown."[4]

While treaties were not negotiated with the Indian tribes, the Spanish government issued grants which recognized and confirmed the lands occupied by a tribe or a pueblo and described the boundaries in linear measurement or otherwise. The right of the native group to hold its land against all comers and maintain its own form of government within the stated boundaries was thus protected. The effectiveness of this Spanish system in guaranteeing continuity of tenure is witnessed by the Pueblos of New Mexico, whose lands and village governments have survived the erosions of time and political and social change since Coronado's *entrada* in 1540.

The northern colonies pursued a different course, with substantially the same results. The English rulers, in granting letters patent to the charter companies which would settle Virginia and New England, made no reference to the Indians residing in those vaguely defined regions, and no instructions were issued as to the manner in which native titles should be quieted. It is hardly likely that the English monarchs were ignorant of Indian occupation, in view of Spanish activities in the New

4. William A. Brophy, "Spanish and Mexican Influences Upon Indian Administration in the United States," paper prepared for 1st Inter-American Conference on Indian Life, Patzcuaro, Mexico, 1940.

World and the explorations carried out by England's own sea-farers, beginning with John Cabot in 1497. The crown granted the land as if it were within the royal domain, and thus shifted to the grantees the problem of coming to terms with the native tribes.

One of the most lordly of all the New World grants was made by Charles II in 1670 to the "Governor and Company of Adventurers Trading into Hudson's Bay," consisting of all the lands that drained into the Bay, an empire whose vast dimensions exceeded anyone's imagining at the time. The charter made the Governor and Company the "true and absolute Lordes and Proprietors" of the region. Acting on this authority, the Company negotiated with bands of Indians, and in at least one instance, by agreement with the Indians in the Red River district (now Manitoba), conveyed land for an agricultural settlement, the Selkirk Colony on the Red River. The Hudson Bay traders, like the French trading in the north country, were not disposed to encourage settlement, which was incompatible with the fur industry. In 1869 Hudson's Bay Company ended its two-hundred-year rule of the north by surrendering its charter rights to the newly formed government of Canada, with the condition that "any claim of Indians to compensation for lands required for purposes of settlement shall be disposed of by the Canadian Government in communication with the Imperial Government; and the Company shall be relieved of all responsibility in respect of them."

Each of the North American colonies in time developed its own rules and procedures for acquiring land and in other situations, often with results that endangered the colony's very existence. After more than a century of the confusions and inequities of diffused colonial authority, the home government made a concerted effort to centralize responsibility for Indian relations, but the habit of independent action resisted and defeated measures offered in the interest of public safety.

The practice in the colonies generally was based on recognition of the tribe as possessor of the soil. The recognition might be expressed in terms of moral or natural right, or it might go no deeper than a desire to avoid getting tomahawked.

The Plymouth landing in 1620 avoided the issue since, as already mentioned, the area in which the pilgrims went ashore had been depopulated by a plague of scarlet fever carried there by fishing vessels or other craft in coastal waters. Explorers had been in the area since at least 1604-1607, when Champlain sailed in and out of the coves and bays between Nova Scotia and Martha's Vineyard. A party of Englishmen wintered at the mouth of the Saco River in 1616-17, the year in which the coastal Indians were struck down by fever. But thereafter, according to a letter written by Edward Winslow in 1676, lands were negotiated for and purchased. He wrote, "I think I can clearly say that before these present troubles broke out [King Philip's War], the English did not possess one foot of land in this colony but what was fairly obtained by honest purchase of the Indian proprietors. We first made a law that none should purchase or receive of gift any land of the Indians, without the knowledge of our court."[5]

The assertion was intended, of course, to demonstrate that King Philip warred without just cause against the colony, but even allowing for some pious exaggeration, the statement recognized that the Indians were entitled to fair consideration.

The Massachusetts Bay Company, instructing the first colonizing group in 1629, showed concern for the safety of the venture, and advised, "If any of the savages pretend right of inheritance to all or any part of the lands granted in our patent, we pray you endeavor to purchase their title, that we may avoid the least scruple of intrusion."

5. Cyrus Thomas, Introduction to C. C. Royce, *Indian Land Cessions in the United States,* Bureau of American Ethnology, 18th Annual Report, part 2, Washington, 1902, p. 601.

The Virginia Company's instructions, issued earlier, also commended expedient action, but only as necessary. Thus: "In all your passages you must have great care not to offend the naturals, if you can eschew it." The colonizers would have to trade with the Indians for corn and other foodstuffs in order to survive, but the Company advised, "This you must do before that they perceive you mean to plant among them."[6]

In other ventures concern was expressed that formal negotiations should take place before settlement was attempted. Thus, Roger Williams visited and held conversations with the Narragansett Indians for two years before he led his associates out of Plymouth Colony in 1638 and settled at the "Towne of Providence." Williams's departure was not voluntary, or at least was hastened by his questioning the validity of the charter by which the Colony was established. In a letter to William Bradford, he expressed the opinion that no king, not even Charles, was "invested with right by virtue of their Christianitie to take and give away the Lands and Countries of other men."[7]

Elsewhere, Lord Baltimore sent his brother, Leonard Calvert, as an advance agent to the Wicomoco Indians with gifts of "English cloth, axes, hoes, and knives," in consideration of being allowed to plant a settlement on the Potomac River. The charter issued by Charles I in 1632 made no stipulation to this effect, but presumed to give the Baron of Baltimore full and absolute powers "to have and to hold" the lands conferred upon him.

William Penn, similarly endowed by Charles II in 1681, sent representatives to negotiate with the Delaware Indians in advance of his own arrival and enjoined his agents to seek "with all possible candor, justice and humanity" to form a league of permanent peace.

6. *Ibid.*, p. 563.
7. Henry Chupak, *Roger Williams*, New York: Twayne Publishers, 1969.

While the Dutch had but a brief career in North America and their West India Company was more concerned with trade than colonization, they contributed to a developing policy of fair dealing. The Company's first instructions in 1625 to the Governor of New Amsterdam, Willem Verhulst, cautioned him to pay for the lands he intended to occupy, and he was to see to it that the land cessions were obtained voluntarily, not "by craft, or fraud, lest we call down the wrath of God upon our unrighteous beginnings." To the same effect, the colonists were "faithfully to fulfill their promises to the Indians . . . and not give them offense without cause as regards their persons, wives, or property."

Since the Dutch in their transactions were responsible for the transfer from Indian to white ownership of some of the most valuable real estate in the western hemisphere, it is noteworthy that they were scrupulous in paying for the land and making a record of it. The first important purchase appears to be Manhattan Island in 1626 for sixty guilders, or about thirty-nine dollars at today's silver prices. This would be about 360 acres per dollar, but since the Canarsie Indians had ample acres besides, they probably considered sixty guilders in European trade goods a fair exchange.[8]

Thus, each chartered enterprise determined for itself, in the absence of official policy, how best to make the initial approach to the Indians in whose territory it was proposed to establish a settlement. Also, each colony in time adopted legislative measures designed to regulate the acquisition of land and the conduct of trade. These measures reflect the same duality of motivation that characterized initial settlement—some actions followed from an ethic of fair dealing, while others were obvious responses to Indian threats of reprisal.

8. Allen W. Trelease, *Indian Affairs in Colonial New York: The Seventeenth Century*, Ithaca: Cornell University Press, 1960, pp. 36-37.

Massachusetts recognized as Indian only such lands as were under cultivation, and as to acreage not cultivated, permitted purchases to be made under license by the General Court.

In keeping with his view that the British monarch could not grant title to lands he did not own, Roger Williams in Rhode Island provided that "no purchase shall be made of any land of the natives for a plantation without the consent of the state." Williams had settled at Providence only after negotiating a purchase agreement.

Connecticut made a continuing effort to overcome abuses as they developed, adopting its first regulations in 1640, and finding it necessary to provide amendments in 1663, 1717, 1722, and 1750. The last of these statutes authorized a penalty of triple the value of the land to be assessed against a person making an unlawful purchase of Indian land, and lands so acquired could not accrue to an estate. The colony continued to be concerned in this matter long after the threat of Indian reprisals had been removed from her borders.

In Pennsylvania another type of abuse required remedial action. Individuals who tried to evade the regulations controlling the purchase of Indian land by negotiating long-term leases had these leases disallowed in 1729. The colony went further still in 1786 and provided a penalty of £500 and imprisonment for twelve months for any person found guilty of unlawfully occupying Indian lands. The severity of this enactment was occasioned by bitter and often repeated complaints arising among the Indians of the Ohio River country, a number of whom, angered by trespassing Englishmen, joined the French in the final struggle between France and England for control of North America.

While a rough conformity emerged in the measures adopted by the separate colonies to regulate land transactions, the control of trade was either neglected entirely or, where reasonable laws were adopted, poorly administered. Yet, as a source of friction and reprisals, the unscrupulous trader with his bag of sharper's tricks, including the use of rum to befuddle the Indians, was as great a hazard as the unlawful settler who pre-empted Indian land. Indeed, the trader and the trespasser in their separate ways were invariably at the center of frontier turmoil.

The complaint voiced by an Iroquois spokesman in 1774 was typical of the experiences of many tribes from the beginning of colonial settlement: "The provinces have done nothing and the trade has been thrown into utter confusion by the traders being left to their own will and pleasure and pursuit of gain, following our people to their hunting grounds with goods and liquor."[9]

A generation later, when sovereignty had passed to the United States, the complaint was still heard, in a letter sent by Red Jacket, the Seneca leader, to Governor DeWitt Clinton of New York: "In our hunting and fishing, too, we are greatly interrupted; our venison is stolen from the trees where we have hung it to be reclaimed after the chase."

Then he voiced the sentiment that must have burned in the hearts of many Indians in different places and at different times. His letter concluded, "The greatest source of all our grievances is, that the white men are among us."[10]

One of the bloodiest of the early conflicts was the Yamasee War of 1715, which nearly destroyed the colony of South Carolina. Even among contemporary witnesses it was realized that the colonists had brought the conflict upon themselves by their unconscionable treatment of the Indians. From its begin-

9. Clarence W. Alvord, *The Mississippi Valley in British Politics*, Cleveland: Arthur Clark Co., 1917, vol. 2, pp. 59-60.
10. John Halkett, *Historical Notes Respecting the Indians of North America*, London, 1825, pp. 310-12.

nings in 1670, leaders of the colony had made a practice of capturing and selling Indians into slavery, but there were many petty ways in which settlers generally, and traders particularly, made themselves obnoxious, such as "killing the Indians' hogs and fowls, gathering corn and peas and watermelons without leave, and paying not half the value, or balancing the account with blows," according to a contemporary report. The report continued, "For a paltry wage Indian burdeners were forced to carry packs seventy to one hundred pounds in weight for three hundred to five hundred miles." Then, when the Indians were away on these treks, the traders bragged "of debauching their wives."

Still another witness cited, as a cause of the war, "the vast debts of the Indians to the traders," generally for rum purchases. The commission in charge of Indian affairs for the colony tried to outlaw the practice, but great debts nevertheless accumulated. "In 1711 it was asserted that they amounted to 100,000 [deer] skins, or more than a year's produce of the whole Carolina trade."[11] The Indians expunged their debts by the direct method of killing all the traders they could reach and came close to driving all Carolinians into the sea.

This was not an isolated instance in which traders, by their unsavory practices, brought trouble upon themselves and upon their communities. The condition prevailed throughout the colonies. All were aware of it, and all seemed helpless to do anything, even when the common safety was involved. William Franklin, governor of New Jersey and brother of Benjamin, characterized the situation in 1764 in a letter to the Board of Trade in England: "The want of union among the colonies must ever occasion delay in their military operations. The first that happens to be called upon postpones coming to any determination till 'tis known what the other colonies will do, and

11. Verner W. Crane, *The Southern Frontier: 1670-1732*, Durham: University of North Carolina Press, 1928, p. 165.

each of those others think they have an equal right to act in the same manner."[12]

Trade with the Indians had always been of great importance in the commercial growth of the colonies, and with the development of Canada and her trade routes into the Mississippi valley the French were rapidly gaining the greater share of the business. With the colonies failing to take common action and in fact competing with each other, their competitive situation steadily worsened. The Indians were alienated and the French profited.

The matter at stake was not the safety of individual settlements nor indeed of a single colony, but the stability of the entire British colonial enterprise. This greater danger was discerned by those who were in close contact with Indian affairs, among them Edmond Atkin who, in 1756, was appointed agent to the southern tribes. Before his appointment he had prepared a report and plan of action, in which he wrote, "The importance of Indians is now generally known and understood. A doubt remains not, that the prosperity of our Colonies on the Continent, will stand or fall with our interest and favor among them. While they are our friends, they are the cheapest and strongest barrier for the Protection of our Settlements; when Enemies they are capable by ravaging in their method of war, in spite of all we can do, to render these Possessions almost useless."[13]

Atkin warned his government of France's growing influence among the Indian tribes, and in his report pointed out some of the reasons for French success in a field in which English interests were deeply involved. The French had centralized control over trade and related activities, used men of training and experience at points of contact with the Indian people, and had

12. George L. Beer, *British Colonial Policy: 1754-1765*, New York: Macmillan, 1907, pp. 264-65.
13. Wilbur R. Jacobs, *Indians of the Southern Colonial Frontier: The Edmond Atkin Report and Plan of 1775*, Columbia: University of South Carolina Press, 1954, pp. 3-8.

singleness of purpose, which was to promote French interests.

His report continued, "The French have accordingly taught the Indians to consider our Colonies as so many separate communities, having no concern with each other. Whence it hath arisen that the Indians in Peace and Amity with one [of the colonies], have at the same time behaved as enemies towards the people of another. Some of the Colonies have made no regulations at all in Indian affairs. . . . Seldom if at all [have they] sent proper persons to look into them. But the management of them hath often been left to Traders, who have no skill in Public Affairs, are directed only by their own Interests, and being generally the loosest kind of People are despised and held in great Contempt by the Indians as liars and Persons regarding nothing but their own Gain."

The details of this historical development have a relevance here, because they resulted finally in the formulation of a British policy based on centralized responsibility for Indian affairs —and this concept, in turn, became the basis of United States policy.

England's position in North America at the midpoint of the eighteenth century was far from secure. Although the English colonial population outnumbered the French, in the order of 1,300,000 to 80,000, the lack of unity and common purpose prevented the Atlantic seaboard provinces from making effective use of their superior numbers. As the century wore on, New Englanders became increasingly sensitive of the French at their backs in the west, building up the potential for driving them from their narrow territorial base along the Atlantic. It was this consciousness of danger in the west that fired the resolve to win the ultimate victory in the intermittent French and Indian Wars.

French strategy in the New World, after initially incurring the hostility of the Iroquois tribes in the St. Lawrence valley, differed from that pursued by either the Spanish or the English. In part, this resulted from a difference of environment, since the north country generally was populated by widely dispersed hunting tribes whose co-operation in building a viable trade economy was essential. Political expediency became another shaping influence and led the French to seek tribal alliances against rival fur traders and the settled communities to the south. Penetration of the continent by conquest or by displacement of the native population was never pursued as a policy. The strategy was rather one of conciliation and the pursuit of mutual advantage. At every meeting with an Indian group, French explorers and traders gave gifts, thus adapting to their use a custom that was practically universal among Indians. They traveled and lived with the Indians, becoming, as the English complained, "more Indian than French." They built trading posts or forts at strategic points along Indian trade routes, but developed no permanent settlements in the interior and therefore made no demands upon the Indians for tillage land. The English record in this regard was striking. According to Leach, "It has been estimated that between 1710 and 1740, the population of Pennsylvania increased from 24,450 to 85,637, while that of all the northern colonies together increased from 184,686 to 510,249. . . . Speculation in frontier tracts developed into something of a mania."[14]

The English were not without Indian allies, and indeed their alliance with the Iroquois tribes, which they acquired along with Dutch landholdings, assured their ultimate domination of North America. The alliance served the English not only as a shield against attacks from the north and from the west, but also as a trade channel through which the great fur wealth of the inland tribes could be tapped long after the supply had been exhausted in the New England-New York settled areas.

The French made repeated efforts to win the Iroquois na-

14. Douglas Edward Leach, *The Northern Colonial Frontier: 1607-1763*, New York: Holt, Rinehart and Winston, 1966, pp. 126-27.

tions away from the British, without success. The Ohio River, rising in western Pennsylvania, offered the shortest route from the St. Lawrence country to the French posts in the Mississippi valley. In 1749, the French moved boldly to achieve supremacy in the area, posting notices on trees in the upper Ohio country claiming the territory for the French king, and building forts at strategic points, including Ft. Duquesne (Pittsburgh) at the confluence of the Allegheny and Monongahela rivers. The purpose was to destroy, or at least to neutralize, the alliance between the English and the Iroquois.

Challenged by these immediate threats, the Board of Trade in England took the first tentative step toward the creation of a co-ordinated Indian policy. It invited the governors of the northern colonies to meet at Albany, New York, for the purpose of negotiating in the name of the king a treaty of mutual defense with the Iroquois nations, some of whom were beginning to listen to French offers of friendship.

The conference convened in June 1754 and almost immediately got off the subject of a mutual defense pact and entered upon a discussion of a plan of union in which all the colonies would be brought under a common government, with an executive and legislative branch. A committee actually drafted such a plan, on which no action was ever taken. The Indian delegates, meantime, sat through the conference and never got to discuss the terms of the treaty for which they were called to Albany.

The Board of Trade was understandably critical of the delegates at Albany and reminded them that they had themselves urged action for the joint management of Indian affairs and for the strengthening of the frontiers, the cost of which would be borne by the colonies. The board then moved for the appointment of a commander-in-chief over all colonial and British forces in America. It also created a northern and a southern Indian department and named agents for each, who "were to be especially entrusted with superintending the political relations with the Indian tribes." The commercial relations were still left to each separate colony.[15]

Some progress toward coming to terms with the Indian tribes on the northern frontier was made in the next several years; Pennsylvania entered into a treaty at Easton in 1758 agreeing not to permit any settlement west of the Allegheny Mountains. The Board of Trade in 1761 issued an order, limited at first to the Mohawk valley in New York, then expanded to include all the colonies, which prohibited all purchases of Indian lands unless approved by the British government.

While the basic problem of centralized control had not been solved, it was under study. Various plans were submitted—by Sir William Johnson, superintendent for the Northern Department, by Edmond Atkin, as noted, and by others. The Board of Trade studied these through the spring and summer of 1763 and prepared memoranda for further study and discussion.

Meantime, the Indians in the Ohio River country had no knowledge that their grievances were under consideration. They were growing apprehensive. The news that France had capitulated in 1760 spread through the forests and down the waterways. The Indians were stunned. Some of the Ohio tribes had been the allies of the French for a century or more. They could not believe that their father, the French king, had agreed to move out and let his enemies, the English, move in. French traders still residing in the region did what they could to keep suspicion and animosity alive. They repeated rumors that it was the plan of the English to drive out all the Indians from their accustomed hunting and planting grounds and to replace them with English farmers.

Discontent rose still higher when the Indians discovered that they could not go to an English trading or military post and obtain supplies on credit and friendly gifts, as had been the cus-

15. George L. Beer, *British Colonial Policy*, p. 254.

tom of the French. The English were especially cautious about giving out powder and shot, on which the Indians had come to depend for their subsistence hunting. General Amherst, commander of British and colonial forces, was insistent on this point. He had no interest in keeping the Indians alive.

Finally, the Indians had visual evidence of English intentions. Teams of surveyors were crossing the mountains, followed by settlers taking over lands they had purchased from land companies. These companies, with grants issued under various circumstances, sometimes fraudulently, made no effort to negotiate with the Indians. They sold the land, and after that it was strictly the affair of the settler whether he survived the wrath of the Indians whose lands were involved.

Then, in May 1763, while the gentlemen in London read their memoranda and held their discussions, the Ottawa leader Pontiac and his confederation of northern tribes hurled themselves at Detroit, the strongest fort in the west. He had planned a surprise attack, which misfired when the post commander was warned in advance. The gates were closed against him, and Pontiac had to be satisfied with organizing a siege, a new experience for Indian fighters.

In spite of this initial setback to his plans, Pontiac's successes were astonishing. In a matter of days after the assault on Detroit, some twelve or fifteen tribes with no previous experience of joint effort against a common enemy, struck along 1000 miles of forest and water trails. By early summer they had captured fortified posts at Sandusky on Lake Erie, St. Joseph in southwestern Michigan, Miami near the present Fort Wayne, Indiana, Ouiatenon on the Wabash River, Michiliimackinac in the straits between Lake Huron and Lake Michigan, and Venango, LaBoeuf, and Presqu'Isle, all north of modern Pittsburgh. Fort Pitt was under siege as well as Detroit. Pontiac held on until the end of October, when he received confirmation of an earlier report that the French king would not come to his assistance. The other tribes had returned to their homes after their initial successes, and Pontiac followed after them.[16]

First word of the Pontiac uprising reached London during the summer, but still the leisurely discussions and exchanges went on. As the news grew more alarming, the pace quickened, but never became hurried. On October 7, 1763, the king finally signed the Royal Proclamation, defining the rights of the Indians in their land. Then the matter became urgent, and the New York packet's sailing was delayed until copies should come from the printer.

The Proclamation of 1763 is, in its way, a confirmation of what had been declared by the Spaniards more than two centuries earlier—that the Indians were the true owners of the land they occupied, and it should not be taken from them except in fair trade. Spain never wholly succeeded in maintaining her position against the demands of her own venturing people—and the question now was, would the men in the north succeed any better?

In brief, the Proclamation declared that (1) the Indians were entitled to occupy their lands without molestation and it established the Appalachian watershed as the dividing line between the settlements and the Indian country; (2) persons who either willfully or inadvertently had taken up land not yet ceded by the Indians must remove themselves; and (3) no land purchases in future would be lawful unless acomplished in a public meeting of representatives of the crown and the interested Indians.

Now the Board of Trade moved promptly to make the Proclamation effective. It proposed the creation of an Imperial Department of Indian Affairs, independent of the military and the colonial governments, with power to regulate trade with the Indians, to maintain law and order at the trading posts, and to prevent unlawful entry upon Indian lands.

16. Alvin Josephy, Jr., *The Patriot Chiefs: A Chronicle of American Indian Leadership*, New York: The Viking Press, 1961, pp. 95-128.

It was estimated that the administration of the department would require an annual outlay of £20,000, which would be raised through a levy on the fur trade. There the proposal became snagged. The question of taxation was being hotly debated in the colonies and in Parliament, and the ministers did not press for action on the Indian question.

After more than a year of stalemate the matter was dropped. The Board of Trade later issued instructions, in which the regulating of trade was restored to the colonies, and this moved the Governor of Georgia to write to John Stuart, superintendent for the southern Indians, "I really most heartily wish that the whole had been expressly taken from the governors and vested in you, so little do I desire to interfere with you . . . or have anything to do with Indian affairs."[17]

The governors of Virginia and Pennsylvania were also instructed to enforce a strict observance of the Appalachian boundary, but when General Gage sent a detachment of troops to turn back trespassers hurrying into the Ohio River valley, the detachment found the task impossible of accomplishment. An army was needed to cover the ground. The net result was to leave matters approximately where they had been a decade earlier.

The pressure on the frontier mounted sharply after the capitulation of France and the breakup of Pontiac's confederation of tribes. The Indians could not hope to hold out against the racing settlers, but they yielded each inch stubbornly.

When the gentle Moravians arrived on the banks of the Muskingum River, where they had been invited by Delaware and Wyandot Indians to establish a mission station, and proposed to lay out a plot on which they could raise their own food,

17. Helen Louise Shaw, "British Administration of the Southern Indians, 1756-1783," dissertation presented to the faculty of Bryn Mawr College, 1931, p. 42.

they were promptly called before the council and interrogated:

> Brother! Last year you asked our leave to come and live with
> us; for the purpose of instructing us and our children; to
> which we consented; and now being come, we are glad to see
> you. Brother! It appears to us that you must since have
> changed your mind; for instead of instructing us or our
> children, you are cutting down trees on our land; you have
> marked out a large spot of ground for a plantation, as the
> white people do everywhere . . . and the next thing will
> be, that a fort will be built. . . . Our country will be claimed
> by the white people, and we driven further back, as has been
> the case ever since the white people came.

The Moravians explained that they intended only to raise
their own bread, and they thought for that purpose a plot of
three acres would suffice. They protested, "Of your land I do
not want a foot; neither will my raising a sufficiency of corn
and vegetables on your land . . . give me or any other person
a claim on your land."

The Indians retired to give this some thought. When they re-
sumed the discussion a little later, they were prepared with an
answer:

> Brother! You say that you are come at the instigation of the
> Great Spirit to teach and to preach to us. So also say the
> priests at Detroit, whom our father, the French, has sent
> among his Indian children. Well, this being the case, you,
> as a preacher, want no more land than those do; who are
> content with a garden plot to plant vegetables and pretty
> flowers. . . .
>
> Brother! As you are in the same station and employ with
> those preachers we allude to, and as we never saw any of
> them cut down trees and till the ground to get a livelihood
> . . . we are agreed to give you a garden spot, even a larger
> spot of ground than those have at Detroit. It shall measure

fifty steps each way; and if it suits you, you are at liberty to plant therein what you please.[18]

In December 1773 it was reported that 60,000 settlers were on the Ohio, between Pittsburgh and the river's mouth.

A dispute between Pennsylvania and Virginia involving the claims of rival land companies over the ownership of land at the junction of the Allegheny and Monongahela rivers erupted in 1774 in an action known as Lord Dunmore's War, in which the Shawnees were shattered by a force of 2000 Virginians. As a result of this defeat, the Shawnees yielded their hunting grounds on the south bank of the Ohio River, and Kentucky was open for white settlement.

This was one of the final acts in the colonial drama, which opened on an idyllic scene of Europeans admiring a "loving people, without covetousness"; moved on to a definition of the rights of these "loving" people in the lands comprising their native world; then foundered on the problem of creating a defense of those rights.

It was the misfortune of the New World inhabitants to have been "discovered" at a time when the major European nations were devising the strategies of colonialism and building the industrial machine that made colonial exploitation profitable. The competition for raw materials which characterized and indeed motivated industrial growth allowed no latitude for concessions to humane principles. Any political power that was not prepared to override scruple where native people were concerned might find itself out of the race for pre-eminence in the market.

It can be said, in extenuation, that discovery of a new world and an unexpected race of men was an experience for which there were no precedents in custom or law. A pope tried to set the moral tone for the encounter. Various statesmen and jurists

18. Paul A. W. Wallace, *Thirty Thousand Miles with John Hecke-welder*, Philadelphia: University of Pennsylvania Press, 1956, pp. 42-43.

tried to define limitations and obligations incumbent upon the parties. But the coming together of men of different cultures and different versions of reality posed challenges which remain among the unresolved problems of the modern world.

It was of this historical phenomenon that Lewis Hanke wrote, "The hostility of those who have power toward those who can be called inferior because they are different—because they are others, the strangers—has been a historical constant. Indeed, at times it seems to be the dominant theme in human history."[19]

19. Lewis Hanke, "Indians and Spaniards in the New World: A Personal View," in Howard Peckham and Charles Gibson, eds., *Attitudes of Colonial Powers Toward the American Indian*, Provo: University of Utah Press, 1969, p. 13.

3 THE FORMATIVE YEARS

For the Indians residing within the boundaries of the new nation, the transfer of sovereignty from a monarchy to a republican form of government had no immediate significance. Both sides in the colonial struggle for independence sought to neutralize the tribes by promising to respect their territorial boundaries, and even the Iroquois Confederacy, ancient allies of the English, became divided on the question of helping one white man against another. From the Indian point of view, neither of the contending parties could be trusted, in land matters especially. Political philosophy seemed not to affect the white man's penchant for taking what he wanted.

The war years reduced pressures on the frontier somewhat, and the emerging new nation took special care to avoid giving cause for complaint. Among the earliest actions of the Continental Congress were certain resolutions containing statements of amity and good feeling; authorizations for commissions to travel to the Indians and negotiate friendship pacts; and appropriations of public funds out of an almost exhausted treasury to purchase gifts as an earnest of friendly intentions.

"Brothers," a congressional note to the Six Nations of the Iroquois declared, "This is a family quarrel between us and Old England. . . . We desire you to remain at home, and not join on either side, but keep the hatchet buried deep."[1]

In those first days, departments of Indian affairs were created for the northern, middle, and southern regions—and General Amherst's folly was not repeated. The Indians were offered gunpowder for their hunting needs at a time when the struggling Congress was barely able to supply its own fighting men.

When in 1777 two land speculators attempted to negotiate with the Six Nations for a land cession in the name of the Continental Congress, they were immediately repudiated, and the Indians were given assurance that the men had acted without authority.

Two years later settlers crossed the Ohio and settled on Indian lands. They were seized at once by the officer in command at Pittsburgh, and their buildings were destroyed. Virginia's governor was cautioned by the Congress not to permit a repetition of the incident. Thus, the new nation took its first steps.

In 1779 the policy set forth in the Royal Proclamation of 1763 was embodied in a resolution of the Continental Congress, which provided that "No land [shall] be sold or ceded by any of the said Indians, either as individuals or as a nation, unless to the United States of America, or by the consent of Congress." A few years later, after the federal Constitution had been adopted, this principle was made into permanent law.[2]

On the basic issue of ultimate control in the management of

1. Worthington C. Ford, Gaillard Hunt, J. C. Fitzpatrick, and R. R. Hill, eds., *Journal of the Continental Congress*, Washington, D.C., 1904-37, vol. 2, pp. 177-83.
2. *Ibid.*, vol. 15, pp. 1320-23.

Indian relations, an extended debate ensued. Britain had proposed an Imperial Indian Department, but failed to provide for its financing. The experience of the previous several decades had clearly demonstrated the desirability of centralizing authority and responsibility for the conduct of business with the Indian tribes. Indian attacks on the settlers were invariably provoked by violation of understandings and agreements, and the separate colonies had acknowledged their inability to control these violations.

Even with this common experience behind them, when the question of granting the national government constitutional authority to act in Indian affairs came up for discussion, states voiced vigorous objection. They did not want the "legislative rights of any state" curtailed in this or other matters.

The Articles of Confederation contained a compromise strategy, giving Congress "the sole and exclusive right and power of . . . regulating the trade and managing all affairs with the Indians," but stipulating that it might not "infringe" on the right of any state. This ambiguity was not eliminated until the federal Constitution was adopted in 1789.

The Appalachian boundary which had proved not to be impermeable under British dominion, was not rendered any more substantial by reason of changed sovereignty. With the war over and the citizens of the new nation resuming their private interests, the advance into the west became an overwhelming force, searching out the mountain gaps, burdening the westward-flowing rivers.

In an attempt to control this movement, the Continental Congress in 1787 adopted an ordinance to provide for the organization of the Northwest Territory, to promote settlement, to encourage self-government, and to establish a procedure by which new states might come into the Union. As an assurance to the Indians that their rights and interests would be respected, the Ordinance contained this guarantee: "The utmost good faith shall always be observed toward the Indians, their lands and property shall never be taken from them without their consent; and in their property, rights, and liberty, they shall never be invaded or disturbed, unless in just and lawful wars authorized by Congress; but laws founded in justice and humanity shall from time to time be made, for preventing wrongs being done to them, and for preserving peace and friendship with them."[3]

In the years that followed, the Indians from the Gulf Coast to the Great Lakes resisted spiritedly. The reassuring language of the Northwest Ordinance was not a safeguard against the loss of their homelands; it only legalized the invasion. Under the great Shawnee leader, Tecumseh, a confederation of tribes of the entire middle border almost fused into an army of resistance. A premature test of strength, resulting in defeat on the Tippecanoe River in 1813, blunted Tecumseh's drive to build a united Indian force. Had he succeeded, the cost of settling the west would have been infinitely greater in lives and property.

Though official policy called for the "utmost good faith," the representatives who acted for the United States in negotiating land cessions often displayed willful disregard of the policy. An Iroquois speaks of this in a message to Washington's Secretary of War: "Your commissioners settled everything as they thought would best suit them and be most conducive to their interests. They pointed division lines and at once confirmed them without waiting to hear our opinion of it and whether it would be approved by us or not, holding that our counrty was added to them by the King of England. . . . We are of the same opinion as the people of the United States; you call yourselves free and independent. We as the ancient inhabit-

3. *Ibid.*, vol. 32, pp. 334-43.

ants of the country and sovereigns of the soil say that we are equally free as you or any nation under the sun."[4]

Fortunately, in those early years, the men responsible for determining public policy had knowledge of and compassion for the plight in which the Indians were placed. Among these was Henry Knox, Washington's Secretary of War and the first Administrator of Indian Affairs. To him fell the decision, as it had fallen to others before, whether the policy should be one of extermination or of accommodation.

The executive branch was faced by a growing demand, from the states and from Congress itself, to ignore tribal territorial claims and forcefully eject the Indians from their lands. The argument ran that, in winning the war, the United States had become absolute owner of the soil. The Iroquois had been told this when they came to Fort Stanwix in 1784 to discuss a treaty.

Knox demurred. "The Indians, being the prior occupants, possess the right of the soil. It cannot be taken from them unless by their consent, or by rights of conquest in case of a just war. To dispossess them on any other principle would be a great violation of the fundamental laws of nature."

The nation could not afford a war of extermination, he argued, and such a course was unnecessary in any case. "As the settlements of the whites shall approach near to the Indian boundaries established by treaties, the game shall be diminished, and the lands being valuable to the Indians only as hunting grounds, they will be willing to sell further tracts for small consideration." A system of coercion would accomplish no greater objective in the end.

"The time has arrived," he reported to President Washington in 1789, "when it is highly expedient that a liberal system of

4. Walter H. Mohr, *Federal Indian Relations, 1774-1788*, Philadelphia: University of Pennsylvania Press, 1933, p. 122.

justice should be adopted for the various Indian tribes within the limits of the United States."[5]

The formulation of the "liberal system of justice" was put before the first Congress, which in 1789 re-enacted the very language of the Northwest Ordinance and in the lands section of the Trade and Intercourse Act of 1790 incorporated the basic purpose of the Royal Proclamation of 1763. In these declarations of purpose, the emerging nation chose to act within the tradition of conciliating the interests of Indians and white men which Spain, and then England, attempted to structure into public policy. The tradition would be further articulated in the years immediately ahead.

Justice John Marshall, in three notable opinions of the Supreme Court discussing the Indian position in United States law, reviewed in detail the historic beginnings of Indian-European relations and constructed out of these experiences a series of judicial statements which the courts of this country have ever since recognized as controlling in Indian questions.

Discovery, according to his thesis, gave a nation the sole right of acquiring the soil from the Indians. No other nation could interfere with this priority without inciting sedition. But discovery did not extinguish the rights of the original inhabitants. Their freedom of action and decision might be impaired, vis-à-vis third parties, but they had "a legal was well as a just claim to retain possession [of the soil] and to use it according to their own discretion."

The occasion for this and other of Marshall's opinions was a course of action pursued by the state of Georgia to rid herself of the Cherokee Indians, whose ancestral lands were within the borders of the state. In 1828 and 1829 the legislature adopted measures which incorporated the Cherokee lands as part of the

5. The reports and recommendations prepared by Henry Knox are in *American State Papers*, Class II, "Indian Affairs," vol. 1, pp. 12 ff.

territory of the state and provided for the substitution of state law for Cherokee law.

This occurred at a time when the Cherokee people were making an extraordinary effort to adapt to their uses the customs and technology of the white man. That genius among them, Sequoya, had reduced the language to written form by inventing a syllabary in 1821, and soon a tribal newspaper, *The Cherokee Phoenix*, began publication under the editorship of a tribal member. A written constitution was adopted in 1827, providing for a bicameral legislature, a court, and a code of laws. The people established their own tax-supported schools. They were making over their primitive agricultural practices and beginning to prosper as husbandmen and farmers. The New Testament had been translated into their language.

In these circumstances, the tribe was unwilling to submit to Georgia, and an action to enjoin was brought in the Supreme Court. This posed before the Court the question of the nature of an Indian tribe in United States law. The Constitution provided that a foreign nation might bring action against one of the states, and the Court had to decide whether the Cherokee tribe was a foreign nation and competent to bring the suit.

The Marshall opinion of 1831 ruled against the Cherokees, with this qualification: "It may well be doubted whether those tribes which reside within the acknowledged boundaries of the United States can, with strict accuracy, be denominated foreign nations. They may, more correctly, perhaps, be denominated domestic dependent nations . . . They and their country are considered by foreign nations, as well as by ourselves, as being so completely under the sovereignty and dominion of the United States that any attempt to acquire their lands, or to form a political connection with them, would be considered by all as an invasion of our territory."

The issue of Georgia's legislative authority to supersede

Cherokee law was not before the Court until 1833. Marshall then defined more explicitly the status of Indian tribes:

> The Indians had always been considered as distinct, independent, political communities, retaining their original natural rights, as the undisputed possessors of the soil, from time immemorial, with the single exception of that imposed by irresistible power, which excluded them from intercourse with any other European potentate. . . . And this was a restriction which those European potentates imposed upon themselves, as well as on the Indians. . . . The settled doctrine of the Law of the Nations is, that a weaker power does not surrender its independence, its rights of self-government, by associating with a stronger, and taking its protection.
>
> The Cherokee nation, then, is a distinct community, occupying its own territory, with boundaries accurately described, in which the laws of Georgia can have no force, and which the citizens of Georgia have no right to enter, but with the consent of the Cherokees themselves, or in conformity with treaties, and with the acts of Congress.[6]

Unfortunately for the Cherokees, the executive branch of the government was not obliged, or interpreted no obligation, to uphold the decision of the Court. The tribe alone could not enforce compliance, so while the Cherokees won in justice, they lost in equity. The circumstances leading to the anomaly will be described farther along.

Georgia's challenge followed a tradition of negation that had always been inherent in the relationship between the European settlers and the indigenous people, what Tocqueville mildly referred to as the inability of the Indians to sustain competition with the Europeans. The attitude came to the surface at various times and places and resulted in episodes of slave-taking,

6. The three Marshall opinions discussed are *Johnson v. MacIntosh* (8 Wheaton 543, 1823), *Cherokee Nation v. Georgia* (5 Peters 1, 1831), and *Worcester v. Georgia* (6 Peters 515, 1832).

of land seizures, of forced removals of people, and of the destruction of temples and "idolatrous" images. It sprang from a conviction that native people were a lower grade of humanity for whom the accepted canons of respect need not apply; one did not debase oneself by ruining a native person. At times, this conviction was stated explicitly by men in public office, but whether expressed or not, it generated decision and action.

One of the first men in United States high office to act from such a premise was Andrew Jackson. As early as 1817, writing to President Monroe, he voiced the attitude that characterized his handling of Indian affairs in his own presidential term. He declared, "I have long viewed treaties with the Indians an absurdity not to be reconciled to the principles of our government."[7]

Chief Justice Marshall discussed the nature of Indian treaties some years later, and his view is one that has prevailed in United States courts. Marshall observed, "It is said that these treaties are nothing more than compacts, which cannot be considered as obligatory on the United States, from want of power in the Indians to enter into them. . . . Is it essential, that each party shall possess the same attributes of sovereignty, to give force to the treaty? This will not be pretended, for, on this ground, very few valid treaties could be formed. The only requisite is, that each of the contracting parties shall possess the right of self-government, and the power to perform the stipulations of the treaty."

And he concluded, "We have made treaties with them; and are those treaties to be disregarded on our part, because they were entered into with an uncivilized people? Does this lessen the obligation of such treaties? By entering into them, have we not admitted the power of this people to bind themselves, and to impose obligation on us?"

7. *Niles Register*, vol. 34, March-April 1826, pp. 11 ff.

Of interest here is the fact that Canada never deemed it advisable to denounce treaty-making as an instrument of public policy and treaties continued to be made with Indian tribes well into the twentieth century. In 1870, at the very time that such treaties were under attack in the United States Congress, the Throne Speech at the opening of the Canadian Parliament reaffirmed the policy, declaring, "The claims of the Indian tribes to compensation for lands required for settlement will be considered and settled in conformity with the equitable principles which have uniformly governed the British Crown." The "equitable principles" were those set down in the Royal Proclamation of 1763.

The earliest Canadian treaties were so-called treaties of peace and friendship, usually entered into after a clash on the frontier, and usually they confirmed the right of the settlers to occupy "and forever enjoy all and singular their rights of land," or similar language. These treaties contain no reference to the boundaries of Indian lands, since all lands not conceded to the English were still Indian lands.

During the unsettled years of the American Revolution, the westward expansion of Canadian settlement was negligible, but after 1780 most of southern Ontario was acquired through haphazard negotiation, usually to acquire lands for a specific group, such as retired soldiers, United Empire Loyalists, groups migrating from the British Isles, and in some cases for resettling other Indians. The discovery of minerals on the shores of Lake Huron and Lake Superior accelerated what had been a leisurely and haphazard process, and in two treaties consummated in 1850, the so-called Robinson Treaties, title was acquired from the Ojibwa Indians to all the lands along the north shores of Lake Huron and Lake Superior and northward to the boundaries of the Hudson's Bay Company territory. These treaties had the further effect of establishing the pattern for the later numbered treaties, eleven in all, by which the Indian bands across the prairie provinces and the northwest territories relinquished their ancestral lands.[8]

When the last of these treaties had been executed in 1923, the Indians of Canada had yielded all but some six million acres of land, parceled out among 2200 reserves.

As these figures suggest, the effect of the treaties, and indeed the purpose, was to keep the numerous Indian bands widely scattered across Canada. There was a historical basis for this, since the hunting economy by which the aboriginal population subsisted required a scattering of the people. While that was put forth in justification of the policy, there seems to have been an undeclared purpose not so much concerned with Indian culture as it was with keeping the Indians under control. An official of the Indian Department writing in 1880 declared, "I regard the Canadian system of alloting reserves to one or more bands together, in the localities in which they have had the habit of living, as far preferable to the American system of placing whole tribes in large reserves. . . . Moreover, the Canadian system of band reserves has a tendency to diminish the offensive strength of the Indian tribes, should they ever become restless."[9]

The treaties followed a fairly uniform pattern. The Indian signatories "surrendered all their interests" in a defined area, in return for which a lesser defined area was set aside for their occupancy, together with compensation in the form of cash annuities or goods and services, including twine (for tying up bales of fur), seeds, axes, mowers, livestock, teachers and schools, and in some but not all instances, "a medicine chest to be kept at the house of each Indian agent for the use and benefit of the Indians at the direction of such agent." A usual pro-

8. Alexander Morris, *Treaties of Canada with the Indians of the Northwest*, Toronto, 1880, p. 16.
9. *Ibid.*, pp. 287-89.

vision also allowed "full and free privilege to hunt over the territory now ceded by them and to fish in the waters thereof as they have heretofore been in the habit of doing."[10]

Each treaty contained wording intended to guarantee perpetual good faith. The language varied only slightly, as representatives of the government went about the business of divesting the Canadian Indians of their ancestral lands. In addressing himself to a council of Indians in 1871, Lieutenant-Governor Archibald of Manitoba declared, "Your Great Mother will lay aside for you lots of land to be used by you and your children forever. She will not allow the white man to intrude upon these lots. She will make rules to keep them for you, so that as long as the sun shall shine, there shall be no Indian who has not a place that he can call his home, where he can go and pitch his camp, or if he chooses, build his home and till his land."[11]

The peace commissioners displayed notable foresight in offering annuities in cash. The terms usually provided that a certain sum would be paid to each individual, or each family, for as long as the population remained constant or did not fall below a given percentage of the head count at the time of the treaty signing. If the population declined below that number, "the annuity shall be diminished in proportion to their actual numbers."

In effect, the Indian surrender was absolute, but the monetary consideration was, at least in part, conditional. If disease introduced from the outside carried off the greater part of the population, not an uncommon occurrence in the nineteenth century, Indian land could pass to the government at a reduced cost. Since the idea of the "vanishing red man" was as prevalent

10. Robinson Superior Treaty, Sept. 17, 1860, and Robinson Huron Treaty, Sept. 9, 1850, reported in Morris.
11. Morris, *Treaties of Canada*, pp. 28-29.

in Canada as it was in the United States, the negotiating peace commissioners acted with a shrewdness beyond the dictates of prudent caution.

The transfer of Indian title across most of Canada was accomplished with remarkable lack of rancor. Open hostility erupted on only two occasions—each short lived and not excessively bloody—the first on the Red River in Manitoba in 1870, and the second at Batoche in western Saskatchewan in 1885. Louis Riel, the leader of both outbreaks, was speedily hanged after the second effort, and that ended any further resort to armed resistance.

Not all of Canada passed out of Indian ownership by mutual agreement, however. For a variety of reasons which need not be detailed here, no land cession treaties were entered into with any of the Indians occupying what are now the Maritime Provinces or the Province of Quebec. In British Columbia, several treaties were negotiated in the early years of settlement between 1850 and 1860 involving a very small part of Vancouver Island. In that same period gold was discovered on the mainland in the Fraser River district, and the idea of bargaining with Indians for land cessions was abandoned forthwith. The efforts of the Indians of the province to win recognition of and compensation for the taking of aboriginal land holdings have been unfailingly defeated by successive provincial governments.

While treaties were made with the various bands of the Northwest Territories, the promised reserved areas were never set aside for them, and no treaties were made with the widely scattered Eskimo people.

These failures to negotiate, or to carry out agreements accepted in good faith by Indian negotiators, leave serious legal and moral questions still to be resolved. As valuable mineral and other resources are discovered, especially in the north, the questions become urgent.

In Alaska, that other large body of native American soil, the indigenous tribes occupied their lands and pursued their traditional life at the sufferance of the United States Congress. The treaty of cession by which Alaska was obtained from Russia in 1867 provided that "the uncivilized tribes"—by which was meant native villages located beyond the pale of Russian occupation—would "be subject to such laws and regulations as the United States may, from time to time, adopt in regard to aboriginal tribes of that country."

While the treaty language appeared to extend to the Alaskan natives the status of Indians in the United States, they were at first entirely ignored, as the solicitor for the Department of the Interior acknowledged in an opinion issued in 1923: "In the beginning, and for a long time after the cession of the territory, Congress took no particular notice of these natives . . . and no special provision was made for their support and education. . . . In the earlier days it was repeatedly held by the courts . . . that these natives did not bear the same relation to our government, in many respects, that was borne by the American Indians."[12]

Almost two decades after the United States obtained possession of the territory, some thought was given to protecting the rights of the natives in their land base. The Act of May 17, 1884, authorizing a civil government in Alaska, provided "that the Indians or other persons . . . shall not be disturbed in the possession of any lands actually in their use or occupancy or now claimed by them."

The language was not explicit, and it was rendered even more ambiguous by the subsequent phrasing which read, "the terms under which such persons may acquire title to such lands is reserved for future legislation by Congress."

While the native people were protected in their right to live where they had always lived, nothing in the law established

12. U.S. Department of the Interior, *Federal Indian Law*, Washington, D.C., 1958, p. 935.

the limits of their holdings or defined the nature of their tenure. The anomaly of this situation remained unresolved down through the years, and as settlement in Alaska accelerated after World War II the situation of the natives steadily deteriorated.

By such successive affirmations and denials the tribal people of North America found the physical limits of their world constricted, and with the shrinking of their world there was a corresponding loss of social momentum. Societies which had been highly versatile in their adaptation to place and circumstance in the New World were suddenly immobilized. The people, as tribes and bands, moved into an era when their voices were rarely heard and their power for decision was largely destroyed. The idea of the "vanishing red man," so long as it dominated public thought and policy, easily excused actions which encroached upon the physical boundaries and personal liberties of a people who were to be displaced. Only gradually did it occur to the emerging nationalist societies of the United States and Canada that their native minorities might profit from schools, employment opportunities, and health care. But before such realization was formalized in institutions and programs, the process of affirmation and denial—mostly denial, it sometimes seemed—had yet to continue.

Zuni Pueblo scene in 1879: after more than ninety years, the young man's clothing has changed, but the beehive ovens still bake bread, chili still hangs to dry in the sun, and ladders are stairways. *(Smithsonian Institution National Anthropological Archives, Bureau of American Ethnology Collection. Photographed by John K. Hillers, B.A.E., 1879.)*

The village of Hughes in the interior of Alaska.

The mayor of Chalkyitsik, a village on the Upper Yukon.

Theodore B. Hetzel

Ute woman in front of her house, Uintah-Ouray Reservation, Utah.
Theodore B. Hetzel

A trading post on the Navajo Reservation—in its own way as traditional as Navajo life itself. The horse collars and collar pads hanging from the ceiling testify that change comes slowly.

Theodore B. Hetzel

Dipping sheep on the Navajo Reservation is a community affair. The dipping trough was built by the community and the families of the district help each other in treating their sheep. The dipping keeps the sheep disease-free.

Theodore B. Hetzel

4 YEARS OF ATTRITION

The century following the Marshall opinions were years of diminution for the Indian people in the United States. The land base dissolved, the population declined, and in some areas, as in the buffalo plains, the very means of livelihood disappeared and the people were threatened with final extinction.

The "liberal system of justice" advocated by Henry Knox had been formalized by law and judicial opinion, but it remained to be proven in practice. The fate of the Indian people, as they tried to carry on life in their camps and villages, would be determined by how well the system withstood the pressures of a growing nation.

The first major assault was directed at the tribes still living east of the Mississippi River. The growing national population needed room for expansion. In the southeast especially, agriculture was beginning a spectacular growth, the impetus for which was not limited to subsistence needs of the nation. Improved mechanical devices for handling and processing raw cotton resulted in the production of mounting surpluses. In the twelve-year period 1791-1803, cotton exports from the United States jumped from 200,000 to 40 million pounds annually, and that was only the start.

Georgia, at the heart of the cotton-growing country, supplied the drive to bring about the removal of the Indians from the eastern area.[1] The lands first settled by Georgia colonists were, for the most part, the poorer lands of the coastal plains which, before the application of commercial fertilizer, were regarded as of limited value for agriculture. The Creek and Cherokee settlements were farther inland, where the soils were deeper and richer. These Indian lands were coveted, not only because of their great potential value, but because they figured in a sttlement with the national government. Georgia's colonial charter, like the charters issued to other colonies, made vague references to a western boundary. During or immediately following the Revolutionary War all the coastal states, with the exception of Georgia, ceded to the national government their ill-defined claims to western lands, and in return were forgiven their share of national defense costs. Only Georgia held back, demanding reimbursement for certain sums of money she claimed it had cost her to acquire title or to defend herself against Indian attacks. The condition was eventually accepted in 1802 by the national government, but in the resulting agreement Georgia further insisted that the government extinguish "at their own expense, for the use of Georgia, as soon as the same can be peaceably done on reasonable terms, the Indian title" to any lands still in Indian possession.

Jefferson, who was President when the agreement was concluded, viewed the Indian-white relationship in very much the same light as had Knox and Washington. He expressed this view in a letter to the agent to the Creek nation in 1803: "I

1. For events in Georgia, see U. B. Phillips, "Georgia and State Rights," *Annual Report of the American Historical Association*, Washington, D.C., 1901, vol. 2.

consider the business of hunting has already become insufficient to furnish clothing and subsistence to the Indians. The promotion of agriculture, therefore, and household manufacture, are essential in their preservation, and I am disposed to aid and encourage it. This will enable them to live on much smaller portions of land. . . . While they are learning to do better on less land, our increasing numbers will be calling for more land, and thus a coincidence of interests" will occur.[2]

Looking to the future, he concluded, "Surely it will be better for them to be identified with us, and preserve the occupation of their lands, than to be exposed to the many casualties that may endanger them while a separate people."

This was an argument for accommodation and gradual change and eventual assimilation of the Indian people. It was the very course which the Cherokee tribesmen had set for themselves at about that time.

Georgia's representatives in Congress and her officials at home were not satisfied with a policy of gradualism. A memorial to Congress declared, "The State of Georgia claims a right to the jurisdiction and soil of the territory within her limits." It complained that the national government was not performing on its promise to extinguish Indian title "as soon as the same can be peaceably obtained."

By 1822, after twenty years, the Georgians thought it was time to drop the idea of peaceable means and resort to force, if necessary. The Cherokees, as it happened, had decided not to relinquish any more land. They had ceded land on a number of occasions, beginning in 1737, and had come to the conclusion that they needed what was left for themselves and their children.

Neither Monroe nor John Quincy Adams was willing to force the issue, but this hesitancy vanished when Andrew Jack-

2. P. L. Ford, ed., *The Writings of Thomas Jefferson*, New York, 1892-99, vol. 3, p. 214.

son assumed the office of President in 1829. A few years earlier he had written to the Secretary of War, "It appears to me that it is high time to do away with the farce of treating with Indian tribes."[3]

When Mississippi followed Georgia's lead in 1829 and enacted legislation subjecting the Choctaw Indians to the laws of the state, Jackson, in his first annual message to Congress, took the position that he was powerless to act against the states, and recommended to the Congress "the propriety of setting apart an ample district west of the Mississippi River . . . to be guaranteed to the Indian tribes as long as they shall occupy it," and where they would be "secured in the enjoyment of government of their own choice."

He sent agents to the Choctaws, Creeks, Chickasaws, and Cherokees—all eastern tribes—instructing them, "Say to them as friends and brothers to listen to their father, and their friend. Where they now are, they and my white children are too near to each other to live in harmony and peace. . . . Beyond the great River Mississippi . . . their father has provided a country large enough for them all, and he advises them to move to it. There their white brothers will not trouble them, and they will have no claim to the land, and they can live upon it, they and all their children, as long as grass grows and waters run."

The Choctaw leaders, when they received the message, sent back word that "We have no expectation that, if we should remove to the west of the Mississippi, any treaties would be made with us, that would secure greater benefits to us and our children than those which are already made. The red people are of the opinion that, in a few years the Americans will also wish to possess the land west of the Mississippi."

In confidential instructions to his agents, Jackson advised

3. The details here are from Annie H. Abel, "The History of Events Resulting in Indian Consolidation West of the Mississippi," *Annual Report of the American Historical Association*, Washington, D.C., 1906.

them not to hold general councils with the Indians and assured them that the Indians had "demonstrated their utter aversion to this mode" of negotiation; rather, the agents should use the secret public funds he had provided to purchase gifts for the "chiefs and influential men" and not to neglect "the children of the chiefs."

Following up his recommendation to Congress, Jackson caused to be introduced in both houses of Congress bills providing for the removal of the eastern tribes. While the language of the bills gave only discretionary power to the President and did not authorize forceful removal, it was understood that force would be used if necessary. The Indians had been told, in fact, that the United States would not protect them if they stayed in their present homes.

Strong protests were heard, in and out of Congress. Senator Frelinghuysen of New Jersey ended a two-day speech with the challenging question, "Is it one of the prerogatives of the white man, that he may disregard the dictates of moral principles, where an Indian shall be concerned?"

Congressman Storrs of New York spoke of the fallacy of pretending to remove the Indians for their own good from a community where they had pleasant homes, churches, and schools to a wilderness where hostile tribes would be their only neighbors.

The answer to both men, and to others who argued for the Indians on grounds of morality and reason, was given by President Jackson a year later, following the court ruling that Georgia could not impose its laws on the Cherokees. By refusing to honor the ruling, the President indicated that he would use his high authority only to compel Indian submission.

Opposition failed and the Indian Removal Act was adopted by the Congress and approved by the President on May 30, 1830.

In the succeeding ten years the Atlantic and Gulf states were cleared of the Cherokees, Choctaws, Chickasaws, Creeks, and Seminoles. Some went resignedly, others at bayonet point. Only the Seminoles resisted as a group, and in their Florida swamps fought a war that lasted from 1835 to 1842 and cost the United States some 1500 soldiers and an estimated $20 million.

The Ohio River and Great Lakes tribes were also rounded up and removed, with the Sauk and Fox Indians making a last desperate stand in Illinois against overwhelming numbers. All were moved—Ottawas, Pottawatomies, Wyandots, Shawnees, Kickapoos, Winnebagos, Delawares, Peorias, Miamis, and finally the Sauk and Fox—all were sent out of their homes to strange lands beyond the Mississippi. Only the Iroquois tribes, except for fragments of the Oneidas and Senecas, remained behind. Years later Cherokee stragglers returned to North Carolina. Seminole survivors were found still living in their swampland hideouts. And Choctaws returned to Mississippi. Today these are vigorous groups again, living now in cramped quarters in a land occupied by strangers.

Count de Tocqueville, as mentioned earlier, happened to be on the bank of the Mississippi River at Memphis when a party of Choctaw Indians was crossing over in mid-winter of 1831. He spoke of the solemn silence that hung upon the freezing air as the Indians moved into the waiting boats. "No cry, no sob, was heard amongst the assembled crowd; all were silent."

"They were isolated in their own country," he commented, "and their race only constituted a little colony of troublesome strangers in the midst of a numerous and dominant people."[4]

The Choctaw spokesman was correct in his prediction that the Indians would not find security in the lands west of the Mississippi. Hardly had some of the tribes settled down in Kansas, Iowa, and Nebraska when they were told they could

4. Alexis de Tocqueville, *Democracy in America*, Henry Reeves trans., New York, 1898, vol. 1, p. 448.

not stay. The discovery of gold, first in California, then in Colorado and the northwest, meant the opening of transcontinental wagon roads and later railways. To secure the safety of travelers the Indians were thrust north and south of the lines of travel. New treaties were negotiated, new guarantees of "perpetual" title and assurances of protection given.

The tribes from the southeast—designated as the Five Civilized Tribes because of the progress they had made in adopting the white man's culture, establishing schools, courts, tax systems, and formal governments—they too found that perpetuity had a short life. Several of the tribes, or factions within the tribes, formed alliances with the South during the Civil War, and at the war's end, in retaliation, the victorious North compelled them to surrender the western half of the territory which President Jackson had guaranteed would be theirs "as long as grass grows." The surrendered lands were parceled out to tribes brought in from the north, and the remainder was opened for homesteading by white men.

Not surprisingly, a tone of cynicism entered the discussions of Indian affairs in this period. When a general appropriation bill containing funds to fulfill treaty provisions with several tribes in the Great Plains was before the House of Representatives during President Grant's first term, one member of the House expressed doubt that such tribes existed, except "in the minds of some Indian traders and speculators."

A quarrel had been in the making between the two houses of Congress, brought on by the challenge of the lower house, which insisted that its members be consulted prior to the confirmation of Indian treaties. The federal Constitution empowered the President to make treaties, "by and with the advice and consent of the Senate." Members of the lower house argued that the Senate had grown careless in the use of its discretion. At the moment (1869), eleven separate treaties, requiring an appropriation of $4.5 million, were under discussion.

The treaties had been ratified by the Senate and approved by the President, and the House, which must originate appropriation measures, was considering the funding bill. The members balked.[5]

One member condemned the reasoning that recognized Indians as owners of the soil. "They never owned a foot of land. They were roving savages. They never owned and could not own land. They could not understand the title to land."

Another thought that Indian treaties were a sham and wanted to insert the expression "so-called" before every reference to treaty in the appropriation bill. He declared, "Every dollar appropriated for Indians, tends to prevent the Indians from becoming civilized, teaches them to live in idleness."

Still the Indians were not without defenders. One senator remarked, "When we were weak and the Indians were strong, we were glad to make treaties with them and live up to those treaties. Now we have grown powerful and they have grown weak, and it does not become this nation to turn around and trample the rights of the weak."

Still another senator rebuked those who had attacked the absent Indians: "I know what the misfortune of the Indians is. Their misfortune is not that they are a dwindling race, not that they are a weak race. Their misfortune is that they hold great bodies of rich lands, which have aroused the cupidity of powerful corporations and powerful individuals."

The House members had their way. They wanted to put an end to the practice of negotiating formal treaties with the Indian tribes. The Senate, after two years of debate, in which no representatives for the Indians and no Indian spokesmen defended the historic practice, yielded, with this rationalization offered by the chairman of the Senate Committee on Indian Affairs: "I have been of the impression for years that there

5. The debates are reported in *Congressional Globe*, 41st Congress, 1st session, 1869, and 3rd session, 1871.

was no necessity for negotiating and ratifying treaties with Indians; that all our intercourse with them could be regulated by law, by statutory provisions, just as well as by treaty; that on the whole it was much safer to submit all these propositions to both branches of Congress than to submit them only to the Senate."

Ordinarily, substantive law is not incorporated into an appropriation measure, but the Appropriation Act for 1871 contained a rider, declaring, "Hereafter, no Indian nation or tribe within the territory of the United States shall be acknowledged or recognized as an independent tribe or power with whom the United States may contract by treaty."

The action was not a denial of the Marshall thesis that Indian tribes are "domestic dependent nations" with self-governing powers. The United States continued to respect treaties previously incorporated into the law of the land, and it entered into formal "agreements" with respect to land and other matters. In later years, indeed, the courts would award monetary judgments to Indian tribes for actions taken in violation of treaty stipulations.

Nevertheless, since 1871 it has been United States policy to legislate in Indian matters, not to negotiate, often not even to consult, no matter what effect the legislation might have on the civil and property rights of the Indians. The policy enactment was the recognition of a reality—that Indian friendship and support were no longer needed by the nation come to power.

With this breach in the historic relationship accomplished, the next point at which pressure was applied was the system under which Indians held their lands. The treaties had set up a barrier protecting the Indians in their traditional notions about land and frustrating the normal acquisitive activities of white men. The courts, in repeated cases, had held firm to aboriginal possessory rights and to the terms of treaties recognizing those rights. Thus one opinion reads, "So long as a tribe exists and remains in possession of its lands, its title and possession are sovereign and exclusive . . . Although the Indian title continues only during their possession, yet that possession has been always held sacred, and can never be disturbed but by their consent. They do not hold under the States, nor under the United States; their title is original, sovereign, and exclusive."[6]

Land was not merchantable, in the European sense, among any of the North American tribes. Individual right of occupancy and use was recognized and protected, and under given conditions trespass might be punished. Boundary lines were respected, as between tribes, and between clans or other groupings within the tribe.

That Indians recognized their non-merchantable possessory rights as against outsiders was recorded as early as 1686 by an Iroquois leader, who declared, "It is only by forbearance that I have permitted the English the lands which were part of my domain and for which they have paid me a price and for which they will pay again each time they approach me."[7]

Such concepts were the cultural results of experiences which differed from the experiences of Europeans, concepts that were designed to serve a different kind of social purpose. They explain why it was that, in effort after effort, the early Indians tried to drive the settlers off land which previously they had "sold"; why tribes sometimes turned upon certain of their own headmen and destroyed them for giving away what belonged to the group and could not be individualized. Tribal leaders were also aware of the strategy often used against them by government officials of negotiating with each tribe separately and neutralizing their efforts to combine their forces. This explains what lay behind the appeal of the Indian confederation

6. The subject is treated exhaustively in Felix S. Cohen, "Original Indian Title," *Minnesota Law Review*, vol. 32, no. 1, Dec. 1947, pp. 28-59.
7. Quoted in *Native Rights in Canada*, Indian-Eskimo Association of Canada, Toronto, 1970, p. 54.

meeting at the mouth of the Detroit River in December 1786, an appeal addressed to commissioners representing the United States:

> Brothers: we are still anxious of putting our plan of accommodation [for reconciliation and friendship] into execution. . . . The first steps towards which should be, in our opinion, that all treaties carried on with the United States, on our parts, should be with the general voice of the whole confederacy, and carried on in the most open manner, without any restraint on either side; and especially as land matters are often the subject of our counsel with you, a matter of great importance and of great concern to us, in this case we hold it indispensably necessary that any cession of our lands should be made in the most public manner, and by the united voice of the confederacy; holding all partial treaties as void and of no effect.[8]

The Indian system of common ownership had never been understood or accepted by the white men who settled in the New World. Europe and the white man's civilization had grown to greatness on a system of private property in land, and it must therefore be a proper system for any people.

So long as the Indian tribes could hold the policy-makers at arm's length, as they managed to do through the treaty process, they could determine for themselves what internal controls they chose to exercise over land or other community interests. With that barrier breached in 1871, only the judicial process remained as a defense against encroachment. A countervailing legislative process was needed and would soon be proposed.

The idea of individualizing Indian land holdings was suggested at various times from the earliest days of settlement and was even tried experimentally. The Massachusetts General Court in 1633 authorized the settling of Indians on plots, "according to the custom of the English." John Winthrop spoke in support of the policy. Thomas McKenny, the first Commis-

8. *American State Papers*, Class II, "Indian Affairs," vol. 1, pp. 8-9.

sioner of Indian Affairs (1824), in asking Congress for funds in support of Indian schools, proposed that as Indian youths "are qualified to enter upon a course of civilized life, sections of land be given them."

Westward settlement gathered enormous momentum after the Civil War, encouraged by the Homestead Act of 1862, which permitted the individual settler to obtain title to a quarter section of public land upon payment of a nominal fee after five years of residence. Discharged soldiers and families from older settled areas swarmed into the western prairies to claim their share of the free land. Close behind them pressed a tide of recent immigrants, anxious to put down roots. Out of a total national population of 31,444,000 in 1860, foreign-born residents numbered more than four million, and a large part of these had arrived during the 1840s and 1850s.

The discovery of gold, first on the Pacific Coast, then in the Rocky Mountains, had an explosive effect in a population already on the move. In this same epoch, plans for the construction of transcontinental railroads were pushed both inside and outside of Congress. The promoters sought, and obtained, grants of public land along their projected rights-of-way as a means of financing road construction.

All of these pressures, in their separate and combined effect, resulted in demands to reduce Indian land holdings, to move Indian populations out of the path of westward migration. The device by which this would be accomplished was an act of Congress adopted in 1887, called the General Allotment Act, or the Dawes Act.

Not that the legislation was proposed and justified as a legal means of driving Indians from their homes. It was not the gold miners or the railway promoters who appeared in the halls of Congress or wrote articles for the press in support of the measure. The advocacy, often emotionally charged, came from responsible public officials, from civic and religious bodies, and from organizations chartered to promote and protect Indian interests.

Carl Schurz, the intellectual political refugee of the collapsed German revolution of 1848 who had become Secretary of the Interior in President Grant's cabinet, set the moral tone of the campaign with his statement in 1877 that "the enjoyment and pride of the individual ownership of property is one of the most civilizing agencies."[9] The Commissioner of Indian Affairs in 1878 reported that the principle of allotment was "endorsed by all true friends of the Indians, as is evidenced by the numerous petitions to this effect presented to Congress from citizens of the various states."

An agent to one of the Sioux tribes expressed the opinion that "as long as Indians live in villages they will retain many of their old and injurious habits. Frequent feasts, heathen ceremonies and dances, constant visiting—these will continue as long as people live together in close neighborhoods and villages. I trust that before another year is ended they will generally be located upon individual land or farms. From that date will begin their real and permanent progress."

The idea had its strong opponents as well. Senator Teller of Colorado characterized the bill when first introduced in the Senate in 1880 as "a bill to despoil the Indians of their lands and to make them vagabonds on the face of the earth."

Later he admonished his colleagues, "If I stand alone in the Senate, I want to put upon the record my prophecy in this matter, that when thirty or forty years will have passed and these Indians shall have parted with their title, they will curse the hand that was raised professedly in their defense to secure this kind of legislation, and if the people who are clamoring for it understood Indian character, and Indian laws, and Indian

9. D. S. Otis, "History of the Allotment Policy," in *Hearings Before the Committee on Indian Affairs,* House of Representatives, 73rd Congress, 2nd session, 1934.

morals, and Indian religion, they would not be here clamoring for this at all."

On the House side, when a similar bill was under consideration, a minority report of the Committee on Indian Affairs protested, "However much we may differ with the humanitarians who are riding this hobby, we are certain that they will agree with us in the proposition that it does not make a farmer out of an Indian to give him a quarter section of land. . . . The real aim of this bill is to get at the Indian lands and open them up to settlement. . . . If this were done in the name of greed, it would be bad enough; but to do it in the name of humanity, and under the cloak of an ardent desire to promote the Indian's welfare by making him like ourselves, whether he will or not, is infinitely worse."

Adoption of the measure was delayed by its critics, but after eight years of intermittent debate it passed into law on February 8, 1887.

Its promises were great, as it seemed to offer what many friends of the Indian people had long been seeking—a formula which would induce Indians to turn away from their own past and accept a place in the white man's society. To make such a transition, it was reasoned, Indians needed to become competitive, they needed to acquire a passion for self-improvement. Senator Dawes, the principal proponent of the measure, was blunt about it. Indians, he said, needed to become selfish.

The essential features of the legislation were (1) the President was authorized to divide tribal lands and assign or allot 160 acres to each family head, 80 acres to single persons over eighteen and orphans under eighteen, and 40 acres to each other single person under eighteen. (2) Each Indian would make his own selection, but if he failed or refused, a government agent would make the selection. (3) Title to the land was placed in trust for twenty-five years, or longer, at the President's discretion. (4) Citizenship was conferred upon all allotees and upon other Indians who abandoned their tribes and adopted "the habits of civilized life." (5) Surplus tribal lands remaining after allotment might be sold to the United States.

The effect of the law in operation was almost exactly what its opponents anticipated—it became an efficient mechanism for separating the Indians from their lands and pauperizing them. In 1887, approximately 140 million acres were owned in joint tenure by the Indians of the United States. The Allotment Act, as amended in succeeding years, set up procedures which resulted in the transfer of some 90 million acres from Indian to white owners in the next forty-five years.

Most efficient in reducing Indian land holdings was the provision permitting the government to purchase so-called surplus tribal lands. Sales could also be made by individual Indians after the initial trust period expired, or as later provided, the Secretary of the Interior could issue a "certificate of competency" indicating that the individual was qualified to manage his own affairs. The Indians' creditors or anxious land buyers could be counted on to assist an Indian in submitting an application and supporting the request with proper affidavits testifying to the applicant's competency.

The lands that went first were the most valuable: agricultural lands, rich grasslands on the high plains, virgin forests in the Great Lakes region. What remained was desert or semi-desert.

The Sisseton Indians of South Dakota, a branch of the Sioux nation, learned first hand how effective the law could be in reducing Indian acreage. The tribe had been moved several times, but finally it came to rest on a modest empire of 918,000 acres. The land was a deep black loam, scattered through with lakes and pleasant groves.

The tribe was among the first to have its lands allotted, and as it worked out, the 2000 members of the tribe were able to retain 300,000 acres, which left approximately 600,000 acres in the surplus category. This was promptly made available for homesteading by white men. The agent stationed among the Sissetons in 1892 composed a pleasant report on the situation: "The Sissetons and Wahpetons no longer hold their land in common. . . . This reservation was thrown open to settlement under the Homestead Law, and today the houses of white settlers dot the prairie in every direction, while a number of towns have sprung into existence, and the red and the white men will hereafter harvest their crops and herd their stock side by side, and when, as the wheels of progress roll on and churches and school houses take the place of the old time dance houses—which last are already unpopular among these honest people—it will be forgotten they were ever classed as savages."

By 1909 two-thirds of the land retained in separate allotments had passed out of Indian ownership. The trust had been removed and the land was sold. Only 35,000 acres remained to the original allotment holders and 80,000 acres had been distributed to heirs, in diminishing parcels.

The Sisseton Indians did not disappear as the land was sold. They used up the proceeds, then were homeless. Moreover, they increased in numbers. The 2000 tribal members who received allotments in the 1890's had increased to 3000 by 1944. Of this larger population, only 500 had moved away, and now 2500 were trying to subsist on a vanishing land base. No part of the surplus lands had been held in reserve for the descendants of the original allotment holders.

A congressional committee investigating Indian conditions stopped at Sisseton in 1944 and reported, "One of the most disgraceful situations in America. . . . People living under impossible conditions, worse than the places in which we keep livestock."[10]

10. D'Arcy McNickle, "Rescuing Sisseton," in *The American Indian*, Journal of the Association on American Indian Affairs, vol. 3, no. 2, 1946.

If the Allotment Act had been proposed as a device for separating the Indians from their land, its successful operation should have satisfied the most hopeful expectations, but the emphasis had been on the educational value of individualized ownership and the corollary value that would accrue from the dissolving of tribal bonds.

The Indians did not become farmers, not of the kind envisioned by the lawmakers. Many Indians had been farmers from a time that antedated the countries of modern Europe. But they farmed to eat, not to exploit a market. In this, they remained unchanged.

Tribal existence became more difficult, as at Sisseton, but it persisted. The reason for this was perhaps best expressed at a gathering of Indians held in Indian Territory (now Oklahoma) in the very year that the Allotment Act was adopted. Fifty-seven representatives from nineteen different tribes discussed the new law, which they opposed by unanimous voice. They explained their opposition: "Like other people the Indian needs at least a germ of political identity, some governmental organization of his own, however crude, to which his pride in manhood may cling and claim allegiance. . . . This peculiarity in the Indian character is elsewhere called 'patriotism,' the wise and patient fashioning of which will successfully solve the question of civilization. Exclude him from this, and he has little else to live for."[11]

What is remarkable about this statement, apart from the anguish of which it speaks, is its clear recognition of the function of "ethnic boundaries" long before the concept entered the literature of social science. It is a plea to the lawmakers of the day to accept cultural diversity as an element of democratic society. The plea, of course, came prematurely, in an era when public policy was generated by a belief in the infallibility of power.

11. Quoted in *Report of the Commissioner of Indian Affairs*, 1887, p. 117.

In Canada, it could be said that there was less official hypocrisy. The Indians, once placed on their reserves, were not subjected to schemes for a further reduction of their holdings. But in fact the original reductions brought about by the treaties were so severe that any subsequent reduction could only have left the Indians homeless. In either case, the native peoples of the United States and Canada were impoverished by their trustees in these years of attrition.

5   A TIME OF REASSESSMENT

The Indian condition deteriorated greatly as the nation prospered. The United States Court of Claims, in reviewing an Indian case at the end of the last century, indicated frank puzzlement. The court found the legal situation anomalous, a situation "unknown to the common law or the civil law or to any system of municipal law. [The Indians] were neither citizens nor aliens; they were neither persons nor slaves; they were wards of the nation, and yet, . . . were little else than prisoners of war while war did not exist."

An investigation of Indian administration conducted by an independent private organization in 1915 reported that "the Indian Superintendent is a tzar within the territorial jurisdiction prescribed for him. He is *ex officio* both guardian and trustee. In both of these capacities he acts while deciding what is needed for the Indians and while dispensing funds."[1]

Over the years Congress had enacted a great body of law, much of it sterile, but some enactments aimed at correcting

1. Bureau of Municipal Research.

specific abuses at the time of their passage became devices for restricting the Indian's freedom of decision and action. The 1790 law which prohibited the purchase of Indian land except through a duly executed public treaty derived basically from the British Proclamation of 1763; in later years it developed into an instrument giving government officials exclusive control over the management, use, and disposition of Indian property of whatever nature.

The restriction of Indian freedom was strikingly demonstrated in 1934, when twelve statutes, dating from the very beginnings of national government, were repealed. These included prohibitions against sending seditious mesages to Indians or inciting Indians to revolt, later used to suppress opposition to government policies. Government officials might remove from an Indian community persons deemed "detrimental to the peace and welfare of the Indians." The President might employ the military to enforce the decisions of an official hostile to Indian interests. Religious freedom had been denied; dances and ceremonies banned as pagan and immoral. School children were punished for speaking a native language.

Until the third decade of the present century Indian policy was rooted in the assumption that the Indians would disappear. Authorities responsible for policy continued to refer to a diminishing population long after the growth had turned upward. Given this premise, it seemed not to be a serious consequence that Indian land was shrinking or that the revenues credited to the tribes from land sales and treaty payments were dissipated in administrative costs and small doles, while nothing was invested in the development of tribal and individual resources.

Then, in 1933, at the outset of the Roosevelt Administration, Congress undertook a radical revision of Indian policy. The reversal did not occur spontaneously. Evidence that Indian affairs had been badly managed became notorious in the 1920s as a result of information made public by official inquiries and private action.

One of the turning points was an incident that might have gone unnoticed, had it not been for the efforts of concerned individuals. The incident involved an attempt to divest the Pueblo Indians of New Mexico of lands which they held under grants originating with the Spanish crown. The situation had been a long time in the making. It began inconspicuously in a Supreme Court decision in 1877, which held that Pueblo Indians were citizens, not wards of the national government like other tribes, because they had been made citizens of Mexico by a ruling of that government when it assumed sovereignty of New Spain. The Treaty of Guadalupe Hidalgo at the close of the war between Mexico and the United States provided that Mexican nationals would become citizens of the United States unless they exercised their option to remove themselves from territory ceded to the United States. The effect of the Court's ruling was to remove trust protection from Pueblo Indian lands, rendering them taxable and alienable. The law prohibiting unlawful entry on Indian lands did not apply. Some 3000 families, representing an estimated 12,000 individuals, moved onto Pueblo land. In some instances a buyer in good faith purchased a presumed title from a Pueblo official or individual, while others filed for homestead entry, in the belief they had settled on the public domain.

In 1913 the Court reversed itself and held that the Pueblo lands were properly defined as Indian country; the Pueblos were domestic, dependent nations under the protection of the United States, and they could not dispose of their assets without the approval of the government. All transfers or entries involving Pueblo lands were outlawed.[2]

2. William A. Brophy, "Spanish and Mexican Influences . . . ," paper prepared for 1st Inter-American Conference on Indian Life, Patzcuaro, Mexico, 1940.

The non-Indian claimants applied to Congress for relief, and in 1922 legislation was introduced which would throw upon the Indians the burden of proving ownership. Failure to establish proof would vest title in the claimant. It was a difficult and costly burden for the Indians to assume.

The iniquitous legislative proposal drew the fire of private citizens and citizen groups, who entered the controversy to help the Indians organize a common defense. Most active in the group was John Collier, who within a few years would become Commissioner of Indian Affairs and a leader in a national movement to reform the government's policy.

In November 1922, encouraged by the citizens groups, all the pueblos sent delegates to Santo Domingo, one of the larger of the nineteen New Mexico pueblos. It was the first time they had acted together since 1680, when they drove the Spanish out of their country. In the name of the newly formed All Pueblo Indian Council, an appeal was issued to the American people and a delegation visited a number of American cities to explain the issue and appeal for financial support. The tactic not only brought about the defeat of the Bursum bill, as the legislation was called, but led to the creation by Congress of the Pueblo Lands Board and an equitable procedure for determining ownership of the disputed lands.

The action served an even wider purpose by bringing the plight of the Indians to the attention of the public. The citizen group, once engaged, found abundant opportunity to use the skills of its members in investigating and publicizing the obscurities of the Indian situation. Such had been the pernicious effects of the policies in force in the previous fifty years that Indians were living in the direst poverty; the death rate was about twice that of the general population; they were heavily afflicted with tuberculosis and trachoma; such schooling as was provided was sub-standard; and few Indians remained in school long enough to profit. In the words of the Court quoted above, their status was neither that of a citizen nor that of an alien. They were prisoners of war when no state of war existed. Indians were actually citizens by that time. Congress in 1924 had conferred citizenship on all Indians born within the territorial limits of the United States as an acknowledgment of the country's gratitude for Indian participation in World War I. They had not been subject to military draft, yet thousands had enlisted voluntarily. Citizenship was not sought by the Indians as a group; indeed, many leaders objected to the measure when they learned about it, fearing that it might somehow impair their tribal relationship. Their experiences in dealing with the government had been such that citizenship was not a possession of great promise. Relatively few individuals made use of the franchise in the first years after the passage of the citizenship act.

Meantime, the efforts of private groups continued until, in 1926, the government authorized an economic and social study of Indian conditions. The Secretary of the Interior, Hubert Work, requested the Institute for Government Research, a privately endowed foundation, to conduct the investigation. Lewis Meriam and a group of associates were appointed.

The result was a report of findings which, for the first time, provided a detailed and objective analysis of what had happened to the Indian people under the government's trusteeship. A program of remedial action was proposed, which required the repudiation of the attitudes as well as the practices then prevailing. The allotment policy, in particular, was cited to exemplify how the government had failed the Indians in its role as trustee and mentor.

"Not accompanied by adequate instructions in the use of property," the report found, with respect to the allotment policy, "it has largely failed in the accomplishment of what was expected of it. It has resulted in much loss of land and an enormous increase in the details of administration without a compensating advance in the economic ability of the Indian. . . . It almost seemed as if the government assumed that some magic in individual ownership would in itself prove an educational civilizing factor, but unfortunately this policy has for the most part operated in the opposite direction."[3]

Perhaps the most valuable contribution of the Meriam investigation was the formulation of a basic concept of the task of administration which would advance the economic position of the Indians and foster social adjustment. The problems of poverty, disease, inadequate shelter, low educational achievement, and general discouragement all derived from the failure to provide assistance in these related areas. Solutions could not be pursued separately, but must all be part of a concerted effort. Hence the report recommended that "The fundamental requirement is that the task of the Indian Service be recognized as primarily educational in the broadest sense of the word, and that it be made an efficient educational agency, devoting its main energies to the social and economic advancement of the Indians, so that they may be absorbed into the prevailing civilization or be fitted *to live in the presence of that civilization* at least in accordance with a minimum standard of health and decency" (italics supplied).

Until then, it had not been recognized that there could be an alternative to assimilation. Even the tolerant Henry Knox, in urging "a liberal system of justice," assumed that the Indians would be quietly transformed as their hunting grounds disappeared, and he was not dismayed by the prospect; it seemed to be an appropriate solution. The idea that the Indian people might "be fitted to live" within the dominant society without being obliterated by it was, indeed, unprecedented as a statement of possible national policy. At the time, and indeed for a number of years afterwards, the idea was not pursued. It re-

3. Lewis Meriam, et al., *The Problem of Indian Administration*, Washington, D.C : Brookings Institution, 1928.

mained for the Indian people themselves, a full generation later, to plead the case for self-determination.

The Meriam formula was also notable as a repudiation of the philosophy of administration which had prevailed since 1871, when the government adopted the thesis that it could legislate Indians into white Americans. It was a recognition that freedom of choice is an essential ingredient of a democratic society, a freedom that cannot be exercised unless true alternatives are available.

The Roosevelt administration, coming into office in 1933, accepted the radical concept that the Indian race was not headed for early extinction. The population trend had already begun its upswing, and a growing body of ethnological studies offered evidence that cultural survival was indeed extensive. The reforms adopted by the administration were designed to repair some of the damage which had been done, to add to the resource base, and to involve and utilize surviving native institutions and leadership. The new purpose was many times stated —a 1938 summary will suffice here:

> Our task is to help Indians meet the myriads of complex, interrelated, mutually dependent situations which develop among them, according to the very best light we can get on those happenings.
>
> We, therefore, define our Indian policy somewhat as follows: so productively to use the monies appropriated by the Congress for Indians as to enable them, on good, adequate lands of their own, to earn decent livelihoods and lead self-respecting, organized lives in harmony with their own aims and ideals, as an integral part of American life. Under such a policy, the ideal end result will be the ultimate disappearance of any need for government aid or supervision. This will not happen tomorrow; perhaps not in our lifetime; but with the revitalization of Indian life due to the action and attitudes of this government during the last few years, that aim is a probability.[4]

4. *Report of the Commissioner of Indian Affairs*, 1938, p. 210.

The program, which Commissioner John Collier directed, issued as a conscious purpose from the idea of the educational process. It was given statutory support by the enactment of the Indian Reorganization Act of June 1934. The Act was permissive, and tribes had the option of accepting or rejecting it by majority vote. Such a choice had never before been offered, and some tribes evidently cast an adverse vote in the belief that acceptance of the law would entail further submission to the government.

As to those tribes which adopted the Act, it prohibited any further division of tribal lands into individual allotments and the Secretary of the Interior might return to tribal ownership lands which had been withdrawn for homestead entry but had not been taken up. It authorized an annual appropriation for land purchase and a revolving credit fund for economic development.

At the heart of the Act were the sections authorizing tribes to operate under governments of their own choice, either formalized by written documents or following customary usage, and to establish business corporations for the management of their resources. This made explicit in statutory law for the first time the principle, which the courts had followed since Justice Marshall's rulings in the 1830s, recognizing the residual right of Indian tribes to govern themselves.

In this respect the 1934 act was an integral segment of the humanistic tradition started by Spain, advanced by England, and incorporated into the early laws and court decisions of the American republic.

The upward swing which retrieved the Indian population from peril in the first decade of the century was followed in the 1930s by a saving augmentation of physical resources and human spirit. The opportunities offered in the Indian Reorganization Act brought into use the capacity for social action which had never died in the Indian people, though it had been obscured. The start was slow in many instances, since the written constitutions introduced ideas and procedures which had not been part of customary practice. The idea of majority rule, taken for granted in Anglo-Saxon governing bodies, was at first a divisive rather than a unifying principle in Indian groups, where action is customarily delayed until all the people are in agreement, or at least until the dissidents agree to stand aside. Also, in the beginning, so accustomed were the tribes to wait on the decision of a federal official, they were reluctant to act on their own in exercising the powers contained in their portfolios.

The tribes that made the most effective use of their political powers became, in effect, operating municipalities—managing property, raising revenue for public purposes, administering law and order, contracting for the services of attorneys and other professional advisers, and promoting the general welfare of the people.

Other gains were made. The record of tribal operations in borrowing from the revolving credit fund was particularly gratifying. The lack of investment capital, and more seriously the lack of experience in handling money, had been one of the great deterrents to Indian advancement. Credit money made it possible for the tribes to increase significantly the acreage they farmed and grazed—lands which, for lack of capital, they had formerly leased to white operators.[5]

These were all positive gains. Their tribal governments were training schools, and after a few years local leaders began to travel beyond the borders of their own tribes to join others in forming inter-tribal organizations on a state-wide or regional basis. In native America, the tribes had kept to themselves within their recognized territories. Sometimes alliances were made for a specific, temporary purpose and then dissolved. More rarely, two or more tribes might remain in close associ-

5. *Report of the Commissioner of Indian Affairs*, 1948, pp. 371-72.

ation for a period of years. These were the exceptions. When in 1944 representatives of forty-odd tribes came together to form an all-Indian body, the National Congress of American Indians, nothing in their traditions supported such action. The fact that the organization continued in existence and grew in acceptance among Indians, as well as in effectiveness in representing Indians before the public, was a real measure of Indian adaptation when opportunity opened to them.

Taos Pueblo Indians celebrating the return of their traditional lands, including their sacred Blue Lake, by formal act of Congress, August 1971. North house in the background.

Theodore B. Hetzel

The Taos Pueblo Council. For sixty-five years these tribal officials and their predecessors negotiated with the United States government for the return of their sacred Blue Lake and surrounding traditional lands.

Theodore B. Hetzel

At Point Barrow, northernmost reach of Alaska coastline, Eskimos dance in community hall.

Theodore B. Hetzel

Meeting of village chiefs, Tanana, Alaska. At such meetings the natives of Alaska discussed the terms of settlement of their land claims, after one hundred years of waiting.

Theodore B. Hetzel

At Soldier Creek on the Rosebud Sioux Reservation (South Dakota), families eat and talk, while they wait for a dance to start.

Theodore B. Hetzel

Drummers and singers, with dancers in the background, at the University of Chicago Indian Conference, 1961. *(Photographed by F. Peter Weil, The Newberry Library.)*

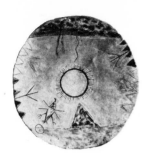

6 RETURN TO NEGATION

A basic debate over Indian policy developed in the years immediately after World War II. The debate was at first a minor play within a general dialogue concerned with government spending and the growth of "big government." It began as a demand that trusteeship over Indian property be curtailed and that some functions of the Bureau of Indian Affairs be transferred to other agencies, but it soon broadened into a full attack on the Indian reform program. In and out of Congress there was an increasing tendency to view trusteeship as a failure. It had not provided a method by which the United States might bring its responsibilities to an end. It had not even earned the United States a good name for its efforts.

A leader in this counter-movement was Senator Arthur V. Watkins of Utah, who as chairman of the Committee on Indian Affairs in the Senate exerted a powerful influence on congressional policy during the administration of President Eisenhower. It was his view that Indians could not hope to have an identity separate from the mainstream of American life, and that those who encouraged such hopes by helping Indians to develop their communities were doing a mischief. He regarded the Indian programs of the Roosevelt administration as misdirected social experiments that perpetuated the illusion of a future for Indians as Indians. He looked to Congress as the agency to deliver the Indians out of bondage and free their property from government surveillance. As he summarized the situation, "Unfortunately, the major and continuing congressional movement toward full freedom was delayed for a time by the Indian Reorganization Act of 1934, the Wheeler-Howard Act. Amid the deep social concern of the depression years, Congress deviated from its accustomed policy under the concept of promoting the general Indian welfare. In the post-depression years Congress—realizing this change of policy—sought to return to the historic principles of much earlier decades."[1]

While this statement leaves unidentified the "historic principles" to which he alluded, the course pursued by Senator Watkins made explicit his determination to restore the process of attrition set in motion during the closing years of the last century. Indian property was again to be made accessible for appropriation; tribal autonomy even in the limited areas remaining was to be further reduced and ultimately extinguished. The concern for Indian freedom which the Senator frequently expressed was in effect a concern to have the United States freed of any legal or moral responsibility for what might happen to Indian people as a consequence of congressional action.

Out of such attitudes held by the Senator from Utah and others in and out of Congress during President Eisenhower's administration was fashioned the policy of "termination," as it

1. Arthur V. Watkins, "Termination of Federal Supervision: The Removal of Restrictions over Indian Property and Persons," in *The Annals*, vol. 311, May 1957, pp. 47-55.

came to be called. Two measures adopted by Congress in the summer of 1953 prepared the way for almost a decade of turmoil that paralyzed community action, destroyed two major tribes, and both frightened and angered Indians throughout the nation.

The first was an act (Public Law 280) transferring jurisdiction over criminal and civil law to certain specified states and authorizing all other states in which Indian reservations were located to assume similar jurisdiction, without reference to the views of the Indians.

Prior to that enactment, state law did not apply within an Indian reservation, and except for certain major crimes, Indian tribes exercised police powers within reservation boundaries. State jurisdiction had been requested in good faith by tribes lacking the resources to maintain law-enforcement agencies among their own people, but the Congress, without seeking the views of tribes not parties to the request, replied with legislation of general application. The Indians protested, since they saw the action as a threat to one of the remaining areas in which they exercised local autonomy; and beyond that lay the possibility that the states would want to tax Indian lands, a power the states had sought for some time. The protest brought no relief.

The second measure produced even greater alarm. This was a policy statement (Concurrent Resolution 108 of the Eighty-third Congress) declaring it to be "the sense of Congress that, at the earliest possible time," Indians should be freed from federal supervison and control. Going still further, the Resolution directed the Secretary of the Interior to review existing laws and treaties and recommend what amendments or nullifications were needed to release the United States.

A suggestion that their treaties might be denounced brought consternation to the Indians, for the treaties, like the land base itself, had acquired a symbolic value with which the tribes could associate their continuing existence. The treaties made them a distinctive people, the abrogation of which would cut them off from their own past. Even the threat of such action was enough to create anxiety throughout the Indian population.

In 1954 Congress moved to implement its policy declaration by authorizing the United States to terminate its responsibility for two major tribes—the Menominee of Wisconsin and the Klamath of Oregon—and several smaller groups. The Menominees and Klamaths possessed extremely valuable timber resources, the orderly exploitation of which provided a sound economic base for the tribal members.

The scale of the decision thrust upon the Klamath Indians is indicated by the statistics of the situation. Of a tribal membership numbering slightly more than 2000 persons, few had progressed in school beyond the eighth grade; a few had received some college training, but none could be classified as professionally trained; even skilled workmen were uncommon. The reservation contained just under one million acres of land, mostly forested. The value of the merchantable timber was appraised at $120 million. A per capita division of this property, if liquidated, would yield an estimated $50,000 share for each man, woman, and child.

By the terms of the congressional mandate, the tribal members, poorly educated and with little experience in money matters, were given three years in which to settle their affairs. Within that brief span they were required either to create a corporate entity to which their property would be transferred for management, or failing that, agree to liquidate and distribute the assets. Refusal on their part only meant that the Secretary of the Interior would make the decision for them. In either event, regardless of who made the decision, at the end of three years the trusteeship exercised by the United States would terminate. The Indians protested at every stage as the legislation progressed through Congress, without affecting the outcome. The three-year period was extended when it became apparent that the required procedures would not be consummated in the allotted time, but the postponement did not diminish the consequences of terminating the trust responsibility.

The question of choice was finally submitted to a tribal plebiscite. Enticed by the prospect of quick wealth, and seeing no alternative, 77 per cent of the adult tribal members voted for liquidation. When it was realized that payment of their pro rata shares to some 1600 members would entail the immediate marketing of 3.5 billion board feet of timber, the Pacific northwest lumber industry protested anxiously. Among the protesters were business and civic leaders who previously had urged the government to release the Indians from trust protection and allow them to control their own affairs. But when these leaders realized that their own economic welfare might be jeopardized by the policy they had advocated, they urged the Congress to practice moderation. Congress then further amended its course by providing that the federal government might purchase the bulk of the tribal estate and, by converting it into a national forest, control the timber harvest. The Congress, understandably, since the Klamath tribe presented no political threat, was responsive to business interests, while insisting that the Indians accept its mandate.

It will be a matter of years, perhaps a generation, before an accurate assessment can be made of the impact upon the Klamath community of the "solution" imposed by law. The immediate result was described in stark terms by a committee of the United States Senate after visiting what remained of the reservation in 1969. The committee reported, "The termination of the Klamath reservation in Oregon has led to extreme social disorganization of that tribal group. Many of them can be found in state mental and penal institutions."[2]

2. Committee on Labor and Public Welfare, U.S. Senate, Report No. 91-501, 91st Congress, 1st session, 1969, p. 17.

At the national level, the Senate committee found that "the fear of termination has poisoned every aspect of Indian affairs, has undermined every meaningful attempt at organizational reform, and has been a major psychological barrier to Indian socio-economic development."

The experience of the Menominee tribe of Wisconsin, the second major tribe to be subjected to the congressional dismantling process, added to the uncertainty and fear encountered by the same Senate committee. The Menominee was one of three tribes at the beginning of the Eisenhower administration that was able to pay its own cost of administration. The tribally owned sawmill not only manufactured lumber but provided employment for tribal members in the woods and in the milling operation. The tribe contracted for its own health services at a local private hospital. It paid the cost of most of its own welfare needs which, because of the job opportunities at its lumber mill, were less than those of neighboring communities. It had maintained through a relatively long history of contact with traders, missionaries, and government functionaries a strong tradition of independence.

In 1951 the tribe won from the government a judgment of some $8 million as compensation for mismanagement of the tribal forest. The money award was paid into the United States Treasury—a circumstance that was to have disastrous consequences for the Menominees. They could obtain their money only by a congressional appropriation, and when tribal officials appeared in Washington to present their request, they found Senator Watkins of Utah standing in the way.

The money would be paid to them, they were told, only if the tribe agreed to legislation which would terminate the trust relationship and free the United States of future responsibility.

The question was eventually submitted to a vote of the membership, in circumstances which almost predetermined the decision. Individual Menominees, in need of ready money, were anxious to obtain their per capita share of the award. The tribe also had planned to make improvements in the sawmill, to expand community services and employment opportunities, and to modernize the local hospital facility. All of these reasons served to persuade the tribal members that unless they complied with Senator Watkins's ultimatum, their court-awarded funds would be denied them indefinitely. They voted for termination.

The resulting legislation, adopted in 1954, set impossible deadlines, as did the legislation for the Klamath tribe, and this resulted in hasty decisions, premature agreements, and mounting tensions.

One of the terms required the Menominees to decide whether the reservation area should be divided into several parts and annexed to adjoining counties or whether it should remain an integrated territory with status as a county in the state of Wisconsin. The latter choice, which the tribal members preferred, required authorizing legislation by the state. This was granted in 1961, but neither the tribe nor the state was able, within the time allowed, to study in depth the consequences of such a move.

It soon became evident that the new county lacked an adequate revenue base to meet the cost of public services. To keep solvent, the tribe, now operating as Menominee Enterprises, Inc., sold cottage sites to summering visitors who found the Menominee woods and lakes a refreshing change from sweltering in their city homes. In this fashion, land once held in common by the tribe passed out of Indian ownership and the Menominees found themselves providing menial labor for the "cottagers" who displaced them.

The tribal sawmill, now operated as a revenue-producing enterprise, installed automatic machinery that eliminated jobs and reduced the payroll. This in turn increased the number of unemployed and the welfare load, at a time when the new county was already in financial difficulty.

What was probably the severest shock to the Menominee people was the loss of control in the management of their community. Their government had consisted of a general council, what in another society would be termed a village or town council, composed of all adult citizens, with officers elected in open meeting. It was a public forum, in which the problems and concerns of the people were openly discussed.

This traditional institution was replaced by Menominee Enterprises, Inc., as noted above, control of which was placed in a nine-man board of directors, five of whom were to be outsiders. Membership on the board was determined by an intermediary seven-man "voting trust," not directly by tribal members, and the voting trust in fact managed the property and was the primary decision-maker. Control was further removed from the Menominee people by transferring to a private trust company the control and management of the shares owned by minors and incompetents. Since this group constituted approximately 20 per cent of the tribal population, the private bank by voting its entrusted shares as a block effectively controlled Menominee Enterprises. The adult members, having scattered to surrounding urban centers in search of employment, left an open field for outside manipulation.

A student of Menominee affairs, after reviewing these events in detail and noting how the people were driven into opposing camps as they faced precipitated issues, observed, "Experienced leaders, young intellectuals with new ideas, potential leaders with experiences outside the colonial situation that could be put to good use, and the Menominee people as a whole are prevented from getting together. The social damage done the Menominees by termination is fully as great or greater than the substantial, quantifiable material damage."[3]

Such were the consequences for two tribes of the "full free-

3. Nancy Oestreich Lurie, "Applied Anthropology," unpublished paper, June 1971.

dom" policy imposed upon them by the Senator from Utah. The ultimate destruction of Indian property holdings and social cohesion must certainly have resulted if the policy had been extended to all tribes, as was contemplated by the authors of the Concurrent Resolution.

The Secretary of the Interior during that period, in full accord with the congressional mandate, moved purposefully to abandon trusteeship even where Congress had not legislated. By lifting restrictions on individual Indian allotments—a procedure that had been severly restricted during the Collier administration—land was allowed to pass out of Indian ownership at a rate that threatened disaster.

Senator Murray of Montana became so disturbed by this departure from previous policy that he called upon the Secretary in May 1958 to halt the process until its effects upon the Indian economy could be studied. It was then discovered that land had been taken out of trust, and invariably sold, at an accelerating rate. More than 2.5 million acres were disposed of during the ten-year period 1948-57, but 1.8 million acres of this total had gone on the market during the years 1953-57. The lands sold were usually the most desirable tracts, controlling a water source or other key feature, the loss of which adversely affected the surrounding Indian community.[4]

A retired field officer of the Bureau of Indian Affairs, commenting on this development, observed, "Tribal officials in the Dakota country are deeply concerned about the loss of Indian land. They know that when an individual has sold his land and used up his money, he does not stop being an Indian. He simply becomes a landless Indian."[5]

4. Committee on Indian and Insular Affairs, *Indian Land Transactions: An Analysis of the Problem and Effects of Our Vanishing Indian Land Base, 1948-57,* 85th Congress, 2nd session, 1958.
5. W. O. Roberts, "The Vanishing Homeland," in *Indian Affairs,* newsletter of the Association of American Indian Affairs, New York, Jan. 1957.

Fortunately, legislative detribalization proceeded no further. After two years of hearings and debates in Congress, the drive lost momentum. In that interval a considerable section of public opinion had rallied to the side of the Indians, and the Indians themselves recovered from their initial shock and spoke out. These Indian protests added to the growing disillusionment with the Eisenhower administration, which produced changes in the political composition of Congress following the elections of 1956, 1958, and 1960. When Senator Watkins lost his Senate seat in 1958, the Indian people all across the nation shared a sense of reprieve.

A bureaucracy is rarely responsive to a climate of opinion and yields to change only under compulsion. In this instance, the Bureau of Indian Affairs, having embarked upon a program of divesting itself of the responsibility of stewardship, persisted in furthering the alienation of Indian land and in denying credit loans for the development of Indian property. When a new Secretary of the Interior in 1958 declared, "No Indian tribe or group should end its relationship with the federal government unless such tribe or group has clearly demonstrated—first, that it understands the plan . . . and second, that the tribe or group affected concurs in and supports the plan proposed"[6]—officials of the Bureau ignored the pronouncement of their senior officer. For a while longer the rule of negation prevailed.

6. Fred A. Seaton, in a radio broadcast of Sept. 1958.

7 THE TRIBAL WORLD

In their resistance to the policy of withdrawing or terminating federal responsibility, the Indian tribes were not expressing a desire to continue indefinitely in a state of dependency, although an obdurate Senator Watkins might make that charge. They would not acknowledge themselves to be dependent in any respect. The protection of their lands and of their right of community control, which outsiders took as evidence of backwardness, was seen by Indians as a contractual relationship not terminable by unilateral decision. And with respect to their trust-held lands and tribal governments, Indian leaders had for some years been urging the federal government to relax its restrictive controls and permit greater participation in planning and decision-making. This, of course, was the promise of the Indian Reorganization Act.

Resistance went deeper. It had to do with psychological readiness and the realities of the inner life which Indians share among themselves. By mid-century most Indians of the United States and Canada had had extended contact with the society beyond their traditional boundaries, and this experience had been varied. Some adjusted to the dominant society in a positive and useful way. Others, by far the greater number, were satisfied with a mixed participant-observer relationship and limited their contacts to the traders, missionaries, teachers, government people, and casual visitors who came across their horizon. Even among the few who succeeded in making the transition to urban life, only rarely was the tie of relatedness completely and finally severed. They tended to commute between the traditional world and the impersonal urban world. This was one of the realities of Indian existence. It had nothing to do with government subsidies or government control over tribal resources. The termination of trusteeship would add to the difficulties of maintaining a community intact, as the Menominees discovered, but the reality would continue to influence response.

The lack of readiness in the Indian people is often charged to the failure of government to provide enough of the right kind of schooling. The criticism would have greater validity if, by itself, the "right" education could accomplish what the critics expected of it. As early as 1609 the Englishman Robert Gray, writing on the bright prospects of colonizing Virginia and civilizing the natives, declared, "It is not the nature of men, but the education of men, which makes them barbarous and uncivil, and therefore change the education of men, and you shall see that their nature will be greatly rectified and corrected."[1]

For the seventeenth-century European so recently brought to awareness of non-European societies, Gray's concept of the process of human development is understandable, perhaps defensible. But as a basis for policy and action, which it became, it was a pernicious denial of the moral right of indigenous societies to perpetuate themselves. To "rectify" and to "correct" in this formula was to "Europeanize." Members of a native

1. Quoted in Roy Harvey Pearce, *The Savages of America*, Baltimore: Johns Hopkins University Press, 1953, p. 10.

community might desire to improve their knowledge and skills, to extend their control over the environment—as Indians demonstrated by quickly adopting the horse, steel tools, and the gun—but the only choice allowed under the formula was to move out of the community entirely; they could not become better Indians, they could only become something else. When Indians resisted and continued to function in a society of their own kinsmen, they were answered with more coercive and more encompassing "educational" devices, until they were wholly encumbered by alien controls.

Governments, of course, agreed with their critics, and in response to criticism they did more of what they had been doing, without discovering why they had so little success with their educational policy. When the nature of the Indian was not rectified, the administration, the men, and the method came under attack. No one challenged the philosophy. By keeping intact the invisible boundary which permitted them to recognize who they were and how to respond to each other, the Indian people evaded the ultimate assimilation intended for them.

The failures of the so-called termination policy, as so grossly experienced by the Klamath and Menominee tribes, produced counter movements, both in the United States and in Canada, which revealed how vital and deep-running was the tribal view of self.

The year 1961 was a kind of watershed in Indian affairs. First of all, there was a new national administration, led by the youthful and spirited President Kennedy. In one of the early actions of the administration, the new Secretary of the Interior, Stewart Udall, appointed a task force which toured the Indian country extensively, listened to old complaints and bright new proposals, and by mid-summer issued a report which disparaged without clearly disavowing termination as an objective and urged a program of "maximum development" of reservation resources. A private study, sponsored by the Fund for the Republic, covered much the same ground and reached similar equivocal conclusions about the destructive efforts of the Eisenhower termination legislation. This report did, however, contain an ominous reminder: "Repeatedly in the past, congressional action in such matters has cost the United States large sums in the later settling of claims or in defending law suits. Error or oversight in a termination today may tomorrow call for the payment of unanticipated indemnities."[2]

An event in that same summer had possibly greater significance for the Indian people than the courses pursued by government. This was a conference convened by the University of Chicago and participated in by almost 500 Indians from all parts of the nation, including Alaska, and observers from Canada and Mexico. A Declaration of Indian Purpose was issued at the end of a week of discussion, and while the document was important as an expression of Indian thought, it was the process of arriving at the joint statement which contributed most to a changed outlook.

To understand better the importance of the Chicago conference, it must be realized that Indians do not constitute a monolithic society. The ethnic boundaries which maintain group identity and functions are essentially tribal in nature. Except for the short-lived efforts of the Pueblo Indians in 1680 and of Pontiac and Tecumseh in the eighteenth and early nineteenth century, inter-tribal alliances have not characterized Indian political experiences. The autonomous tribe, or band, or village, which seems best to describe the political constituency, is a projection of the autonomous individual. No Indian individual, even within his own family, speaks for another individual. No tribe presumes to speak for another tribe. To act otherwise is to act discourteously, if not indecently.

2. The quotation is from the *Summary Report* of the Commission, Albuquerque, New Mexico, 1961, p. 7.

The representatives of the seventy tribes at the Chicago conference had in common a sense of being under attack, and it was this shared experience which drew them together. Even in the presence of a common danger, however, collaboration was not sponetaneously achieved. Indians from traditionalist communities were fearful of finding themselves associated with ideas or actions which might betray their interests. Reservation Indians were especially distrustful of their urbanized kinsmen, whom they suspected of scheming to liquidate tribal resources and claim their share. In the absence of traditional channels for inter-tribal communication, the conferees had as their only guiding experience their generations of negotiating with the white man, an experience that had taught extreme wariness and distrust. At several critical moments the conference stood ready to dissolve, but on each such occasion an acceptable base for continuing discussion was found. And so the conference remained in session until it put together the Declaration of Indian Purpose, which a special sub-committee of the United States Senate some years later described as "forecful and eloquent."

The conference was significant not only because the tribal participants found it possible to work their way through divisive counter moves, but out of their deliberations emerged issues and personalities which in the next few years would greatly affect the forces operating in Indian affairs. A noticeable element throughout the conference was the young adult group, mostly college students, who infused a spirit of militancy into the discussions and before the conference ended had taken the first steps toward the formation of a National Indian Youth Council. This group, after some initial awkwardness in sorting out leadership problems, soon became an effective rallying force for young dissidents. Members of the group joined the poverty march on Washington in 1963 and were soon using the term "Red Power" as an assertion of their commitment to political action. In this they were voicing their impatience with their elders, who traditionally withdrew from open conflict and preferred silent opposition or passive obstructionism.

The Kennedy-Johnson administration engaged in a major effort to deal with the problems of poverty, marked by decaying rural areas and exploding urban ghettoes. In creating an organizational structure to cope with critical economic and social derangements, Indian reservations were listed among the nation's most deeply depressed areas, and this in turn led to the establishment of agencies and programs that were without precedent in the administration of Indian affairs. Credit for introducing the fresh ideas and working methods cannot be ascribed to the Bureau of Indian Affairs, however, since that agency had first to overcome the ill will it had engendered by sponsoring termination policies. The impetus for change came rather from other branches of government, and specifically from administrative bodies newly created to deal nationally with poverty issues.

A major consequence for Indian communities was the adoption of the Economic Opportunity Act in 1965, which authorized funds for programs adapted to Indian needs. Among these, the Head Start program provided early education experiences within the home community for Indian children, many of whom come from non-English speaking homes and homes having limited contact with the dominant culture. These children ordinarily spend the first school years in social isolation and never quite catch up with their English-speaking peers. The Upward Bound program, designed to encourage students to complete their secondary schooling and continue into college, was a major factor in accelerating the recent trend toward professional training. VISTA, the domestic counterpart of the Peace Corps, brought youthful volunteers from all parts of the nation to Indian reservations as community workers. The involvement of outsiders in work projects largely defined by tribal leaders helped to reduce the barrier of unfamiliarity which ordinarily insulates an Indian community from outside society. Of less importance, perhaps, were the physical accomplishments of the VISTA workers.

The outstanding innovation of the period was the establishment of Indian Community Action Programs, which brought to reservation communities technical services and financial assistance for which tribes had always been dependent upon the Bureau of Indian Affairs. The Office of Economic Opportunity which administered the new law had no paternalistic tradition to inhibit its procedures, and it invited tribal officials to prepare and submit plans for local projects. Once a plan was approved, OEO contracted with the tribal organization to operate the project, and it advanced the budgeted funds. This transferal of authority and responsibility for decision-making to the local community was an administrative feat which the Bureau of Indian Affairs, after more than one hundred years of stewardship, had never managed to carry out.

The contrast in method did not go unnoticed in Indian communities, where local leaders responded promptly to the opportunity for improving living conditions. By the end of the decade the leaders of Indian reservations in seventeen states, with technical assistance from outside advisers, had created sixty community action programs, each of which consisted of a variety of separate but related enterprises. The major universities of the western states responded to requests for technical help in training community workers and in designing operating procedures. The very tasks which over the years the Indian bureau failed to accomplish, explaining away its failure as a reflection of the incapacity or inexperience of Indian leadership, were found not to be insurmountable. Indian communities quietly took control of their own advancement.

The manner in which the Rough Rock community of the

Navajo reservation in Arizona assumed responsibility for the education of its children exemplified this development. The people of Rough Rock, very few of whom had been exposed to formal schooling and were non-English speaking, were asked to take over the management of a newly constructed school. The Bureau of Indian Affairs, which built the school, was at the point of recruiting teaching staff and administrative personnel when the Office of Economic Opporunity offered to assist the Navajo community in assuming the management role. An agreement was reached by which the two federal agencies would advance the normal operating funds and provide supplementary grants for developmental purposes.

The important factor in this agreement was not the transfer of the school facility but the shift in the educational philosophy which the transfer made possible. The notion that an educational system, devised to answer the social needs of a given culture, could "rectify and correct" the way of life of people of another culture, which had prevailed since the seventeenth century, could now be challenged.

The Rough Rock school was founded on these assumptions: (1) a school must involve the people of a community, not just the professional and custodial personnel recruited from the outside, and involvement must mean responsibility for success and failure; (2) a school must contribute to the development of a community, which meant that adults as well as children should find learning opportunities; (3) a school should be part of a process by which the way of life of a people is transmitted to the young—the school which is concerned only with importing the culture of an alien society robs the community of its natural increase; and 4. a school operating in a non-English speaking community should treat English as a second language to be mastered after the child acquires a basic competency in his mother tongue. These assumptions, as will be recognized, represented a radical departure from the patterns of schooling provided by colonial, then national, governments.

It must be added that these conceptual generalizations reflect the experience and aspirations of this particular community of traditional, non-urbanized Navajo tribesmen; they are not abstractions derived from academic literature. A member of the all-Navajo seven member school board which operates the Rough Rock school expressed very clearly his understanding of what was being attempted. Speaking in answer to the criticism that the school was educating for the past, not the present, and by such backward-looking methods was doing an injury to the children, the unlettered board member declared, "We are not educating for today; we are educating for tomorrow. The way a person can live successfully in tomorrow's world is to have confidence in himself and have an inner strength which comes only from a positive picture of himself. This school is designed not to teach the children to walk on this road or that road but rather to give them the tools to make intelligent choices."[3]

The transfer of authority at Rough Rock was not an isolated affair, but must be seen as an event in a growing movement for self-determination. This movement took various programmatic forms, and in addition it was verbalized in demands for still other programs and for policy changes. In the educational theater, profiting from the Rough Rock example, independent school districts serving an Indian or a mixed Indian and white community were established for the Rocky Boy reservation in Montana, the Blackwater district on the Gila reservation in Arizona, the Tama Indian community in Iowa, and the Ramah

3. The Rough Rock experiment is discussed in a statement by Dr. Robert A. Roessel, Jr., in "Indian Education," *Hearings Before the Committee on Labor and Public Welfare*, United States Senate, 90th Congress, 1st and 2nd sessions, part I, 1969, pp. 12-25.

Navajo district in New Mexico. These pioneering efforts were important as demonstrations of Indian community resourcefulness and equally important in encouraging other communities to negotiate contractual relationships with agencies of government.

The national concern with civil rights in the 1960s expressed in riots, protest marches, court orders, and political debates caught up the Indian cause, not always with complete Indian collaboration. Some of the issues involved in the civil rights struggle were not Indian issues. Segregation, which the black man protested so bitterly, was not seen as a denial of social status by Indians. They had never aspired to a place in the white man's society, except as individuals might make that choice for themselves. What Indians as tribal members desired was the good faith performance by the national government of the contractual obligations and reciprocities incorporated in treaties. In addition to which, since their resources were under trust restrictions and not convertible into risk capital, tribal Indians demanded development funds to improve their communities as places to live.

These represented civil rights of a different order, and to the extent that they were understood as such they found support from citizen groups, from agencies of government other than the Indian Bureau, from within Congress itself, and finally from Presidents Johnson and Nixon. Public opinion generally, as voiced in major news media, repudiated the negativism of the Eisenhower legislative program and encouraged the Indian quest for a continuing identity within the major society. For the first time since the creation of the Bureau of Indian Affairs in 1824, it seemed possible at the opening of the seventh decade of the twentieth century that Indian communities would be permitted to adapt to the necessities of their environment without submitting to conditions that violated traditional values.

As an instance of the new attitude that came into existence among the agencies working with the Indian people is a report published by the Department of Labor in 1969. The report reflected the experiences of members of that department who had been engaged in a survey of the employment needs of the Indian population. With remarkable candor, the reporting team declared, "We grew to admire the Indians tremendously as a group, to marvel at their courage and dignity even in the midst of abject poverty, and to appreciate their lack of aggressive acquisitiveness. Even their reserve appeared to be the symbol of an inner strength as well as an insulation against the deteriorating influence of white society. . . . We realized what a tremendous loss to mankind would be the obliteration of this culture, call the obliteration process what one will—assimilation, acculturation, or termination. We became strong partisans of the belief that the Indians should be encouraged and helped to preserve their culture. . . . This position is consistent with a great body of enlightened opinion in this country, and with prevailing opinion among the Indians themselves."[4]

Two presidential messages, addressed to the Congress somewhat more than two years apart, were without precedent in United States history. Chief executives had made passing references to the Indian people in their annual messages, but none had addressed himself to the subject at such length as did Presidents Johnson and Nixon. The effect of these official communications was to bring the condition of the Indian people to national attention in a manner never before attempted. It moved the discussion of Indian needs and Indian aspirations out of the committee rooms of Congress and out of the private offices of civil servants into the arena of public concern. It had the fur-

4. *Toward Economic Development for Native American Communities,* Joint Economic Committee, Congress of the United States, vol. 1, part I, 91st Congress, 1st session, 1969, p. 125.

ther effect of openly repudiating the policy of negativism and giving support to a policy of democratic pluralism. Thus, President Johnson in his message of March 6, 1968, declared:

> There can be no question that the government and the people of the United States have a responsibility to the Indians.
>
> In our efforts to meet that responsibility, we must pledge to respect fully the dignity and the uniqueness of the Indian citizen.
>
> That means partnership—not paternalism.
>
> We must affirm the right of the first Americans to remain Indians while exercising their rights as Americans.
>
> We must affirm their rights to freedom of choice and self-determination.
>
> We must seek new ways to provide federal assistance to Indians—with new emphasis on Indian self-help and with respect for Indian culture.
>
> And we must assure the Indian people that it is our desire and intention that the special relationship between the Indian and his government grow and flourish."[5]

The Nixon message of July 8, 1970, offered a thoughtful and critical view of government policy—in itself an unusual function for an executive document to assume. The statement was explicit in its denunciation of the termination policy of the Eisenhower administration, in which Richard Nixon served as Vice President.

In presenting this opposing view, the message recapitulated the long history of government-Indian relations. It stated, "Termination implies that the federal government has taken on a trusteeship responsibility for Indian communities as an act of generosity toward a disadvantaged people and that it can therefore discontinue this responsibility on a unilateral basis whenever it sees fit. But the unique status of Indian tribes does not

5. "Indian Record," newsletter of the Bureau of Indian Affairs, Washington, D.C., 1968.

rest on any premise such as this. The special relationship between the Indians and the federal government is the result instead of solemn obligations which have been entered into by the United States government. Down through the years, through written treaties and through formal and informal agreements, our government has made specific commitments to the Indian people. For their part, the Indians often surrendered claims to vast tracts of land and have accepted life on government reservations. In exchange, the government has agreed to provide community services such as health, education, and public safety, services which would presumably allow Indian communities to enjoy a standard of living comparable to that of other Americans."[6]

The message noted further that forced termination, as a practical policy, had been harmful in its effects; it "produced considerable disorientation among the affected Indians and has left them unable to relate to a myriad of federal, state, and local assistance efforts."

In affirmation of national responsibility in this sector, the message declared, "This, then, must be the goal of any new national policy toward the Indian people; to strengthen the Indian's sense of autonomy without threatening his sense of community. We must assure the Indian that he can assume control of his own life without being separated involuntarily from the tribal group. And we must make it clear that the Indians can become independent of federal control without being cut off from federal concern and federal support."

The principal instrument proposed by the President for enabling Indian tribes to become independent of federal control was a system of contractual relationships. He remarked, "In the past, we have often assumed that because the government is obliged to provide certain services for Indians, it therefore must

6. Message from the President of the United States, House of Representatives Document No. 91-363, 91st Congress, 2nd session, July 8, 1970.

administer those services . . . but there is no necessary reason for this assumption. Federal support programs for non-Indian communities—hospitals and schools are two ready examples—are ordinarily administered by local authorities. There is no reason why Indian communities should be deprived of the privilege of self-determination merely because they receive monetary support from the federal government. Nor should they lose federal money because they reject federal control."

Such declarations and affirmations, if projected into law and administrative practices, carry the promise of restoring to the tribal world the capacity of adapting to change in an orderly manner. A society left to itself normally responds to a changing environment. To interfere with the process by imposing the values of an alien experience is to destroy human capacity—what we have come to know as genocide. To grow beyond the seventeenth century in this respect is the great challenge of our day.

Woman rocks baby in ramada or outdoor living space, shaded from the Arizona desert sun. The Papago family cooks, eats, and visits here.

Theodore B. Hetzel

A motorized sleigh ride for the children at Tanana, the Athabaskan interior of Alaska.

Theodore B. Hetzel

This Cherokee older sister fills a role familiar in Indian societies.
Theodore B. Hetzel

At Point Barrow on Alaska's Arctic coast, children in the techno-
logical age.

Theodore B. Hetzel

At Tanana on the Yukon River, for the children summer comes.

Theodore B. Hetzel

The Neighborhood Youth Corps brings work and learning experience to these Hopi boys at Moencopi village, Arizona.

Theodore B. Hetzel

At Lame Deer, Montana, boys of the Northern Cheyenne tribe
practice the songs of their people.

Theodore B. Hetzel

8 TRAVAIL IN THE NORTH

The Indians of Canada had no head of government to speak in favor of tribal autonomy and community self-determination. Instead, Prime Minister Trudeau declared publicly in 1969, "We won't recognize aboriginal rights," and insisted that Indians "should become Canadians as all other Canadians."[1]

Leading up to that policy declaration was a history of overweening paternalism, not unlike that which prevailed in the United States, but with curiously contrasting differences. For both countries, the Royal Proclamation of 1763 established criteria for the conduct of affairs between Indian and white man: Indian occupancy of the land was to be respected; land was not to pass from Indian to white man except by formal negotiation participated in by government. The men who conducted these affairs, moreover, shared a common tradition of respect for law and the judicial process. And yet, in the course

1. Prime Minister Pierre Elliott Trudeau, speech delivered at Vancouver, B.C., August 8, 1969.

of time, as practice was structured in policy and sanctioned by court rulings, quite opposite purposes came to be served.

The American experience, as we have seen, resulted in a number of adjudications and decrees which set up safeguards against the incursion of private land grabbers on the one hand and against misfeasance by government on the other.

The Congress of the United States set an early example in erecting barriers around Indian land. The Northwest Ordinance of 1787, mentioned above, and later enactments, reaffirmed the British policy declaration of 1763. This was followed in the 1830s by the Supreme Court, through Justice Marshall, which recognized the self-governing powers of Indian tribes. While the westward movement of the nation effectively nullified these first attempts to create "a liberal system of justice," the principles of such a system remained in the legal conscience and were restated from time to time, clarifying the issue and broadening the application.

In *Ex parte Crow Dog* (1883), the Supreme Court ruled that federal courts did not have jurisdiction in tribal territory and could not impose on a tribal people "rules and penalties of which they could have no previous warning." Congress later legislated to extend jurisdiction over Indian land, but only with regard to certain specified major crimes, leaving tribal authority intact in areas not specified.

In *Talton v. Mayes* (1896) it was held that "the powers of local self-government enjoyed by the Cherokee nation existed prior to the Constitution" and were only "subject to the supreme legislative authority of the United States." The opinion here derived directly from the earlier views expressed by Justice Marshall.

Certain land case decisions made explicit the promises contained in the 1763 Proclamation. Thus, in *United States v. Shoshoni Tribe* (1938), the Court struck down the argument put forward by the Department of Justice that an Indian tribe had only a right to the surface of the land incidental to farming and husbandry. "For all practical purposes," the Court ruled, "the tribe owned the land. . . . The right that has always been understood to belong to Indians, undisturbed possessors of the soil from time immemorial." This included the timber on the land and the minerals that lay below.

The question of aboriginal occupancy rights was squarely faced in *United States as Guardian of Walapai v. Santa Fe Railway* (1941). A reservation for the Walapai Indians of Arizona had been created by executive order in 1883, but the reserved area included blocks of land previously (in 1866) granted as a right-of-way for the Santa Fe Railway. No treaty had ever been negotiated with the tribe, hence no determination of the lands claimed or occupied by the tribe had ever been acknowledged by the United States. The Court held that "Indian occupancy, even though unrecognized by treaty or act of Congress, established property rights valid against non-Indian grantees such as the defendant railroad." The railroad company was required to return to Indian ownership 509,000 acres, which according to the court Congress had no right to bestow.

In *United States v. Alcea Band of Tilamooks*, the Court declared that "the Indian's right of occupany has always been held to be sacred; something not to be taken from him except by his consent, and then only upon such consideration as shall be agreed upon."[2]

Performance by public officials, even by the Congress, in dealing with Indian questions was not always in harmony with the high-minded principles expressed in these Court decisions, and tribal groups found it necessary to sue the United States for a redress of grievances. This was a long and frustrating process, since the plaintiff had first to obtain legislative consent for his day in court. The delays were often so prolonged that principal witnesses for the tribe died before the matter came to trial and

2. These cases are reviewed in Cohen, *Minnesota Law Review, op. cit.*

the cause was either lost or seriously compromised. But here again the tradition of good faith finally prevailed with the statutory creation in 1946 of the Indian Claims Commission. The legislation establishing the commission set a time limit, several times extended, within which tribes might file claims for judgment against the United States. More than 800 such claims have been filed, and during the years 1950-70 awards amounting to about $300 million were paid to 101 tribal claimants. These payments represented less than 5 per cent of the amount claimed.

Viewed against this record, the Canadian experience is clouded by ambiguity and equivocations. When Prime Minister Trudeau declared that his government would not recognize aboriginal rights, he was reflecting an undoubted trend in the history of Indian-white relations in his country.

If Canadian policy over the years showed inconsistencies, part of the explanation is to be found in the apparent reluctance of government to assume responsibility for the conduct of Indian business. As a department within the national household, Indian affairs was cast in the role of the unloved orphan. Until 1860, the government of England maintained control and bore the cost of management, whatever that amounted to. Canada, as a province, was given the responsibility, and the expense, in that year. This was regularized under the British North America Act of 1867, by which the Parliament of Canada assumed exclusive legislative authority over "Indians and lands reserved for Indians." Legislative primacy, however, was not an administrative priority.

Actual management was first lodged in the Crown Lands Department, but after 1867 it was placed directly in the government of Canada. There followed a rather bewildering course of administrative makeshifts with no apparent logic. The Department of the Secretary of State handled Indian affairs briefly between 1869 and 1873. For a slightly longer period, 1873-80, these matters were assigned to a separate branch of the Department of the Interior. Then for better than a half-century, 1880-1936, Indian affairs functioned as a separate department, only to become a branch of the Department of Mines and Resources in 1936. Since Indians were not mines and presumably were not resources, in 1950 their concerns were transferred to the Department of Citizenship and Immigration, and next, in 1966, to the Department of Indian Affairs and Northern Development. The Indians had no reason to believe even at this late date that there would be continuity in the relationship they shared with the national government.

Within this shifting administrative landscape, the lawmakers of the nation seemed intent on laying down immovable boundaries within which to contain the Indians of Canada. The Indian Act of 1880, in typical colonial style and in multiple sections and sub-sections, provided that "The Minister . . . may authorize use of [Indian] land for schools or burial grounds . . . authorize surveys and subdivisions . . . determine and direct the construction of roads . . . issue certificates of possession . . . direct an Indian person or the tribe to compensate another Indian . . . call a referendum . . . appoint executors of wills . . . declare the will of an Indian to be void . . . issue temporary permits for the taking of sand, gravel, clay and other non-metallic substances upon or under lands in a reserve . . . make expenditures out of the revenues of a tribe to assist sick, aged, or destitute Indians of the tribe and provide for the burial of deceased indigent members . . . etc." The Act left almost no detail of management to Indian decision or initiative. The only major revision of the Act was not accomplished until 1951, and that did not alter its basic character.

As described in 1969 by Harold Cardinal, the young president of the Alberta Indian Association, "This piece of legislation that was supposed to implement the terms of the treaties was surely written by people who understood or cared very little about protecting human rights but who were thoroughly conversant with concepts and laws characteristic of colonial powers."[3]

However critical they might be of this legislative instrument, the Indians of Canada expressed strong opposition to a proposal offered by Prime Minister Trudeau's government to revoke the Indian Act. The Prime Minister and his minister in charge of Indian affairs regarded the Act as class legislation and seemed to expect that the Indians would be grateful for their offer to scutttle it. In this the government miscalculated. The Act might be resented for its nineteenth-century imperialist thrust, but the Indians saw it as the main body of law from which their legal rights derived. It needed modernizing, but not outright repudiation.

A spokesman declared, "We do not want the Indian Act retained because it is a good piece of legislation. It isn't. It is discrimination from start to finish. . . . No just society and no society with even pretensions to being just can long tolerate such a piece of legislation, but we would rather continue to live in bondage under the inequitable Indian Act than surrender our sacred rights."[4]

These administrative uncertainties, however, were not the only source of anxiety touching the lives of the Canadian Indians. Large segments of the Indian population lived in areas not defined and guaranteed by treaty, and the treaties themselved where they existed were coming under attack as having outlived their usefulness. In the same 1969 speech in which he questioned the validity of aboriginal rights, the Prime Minister stated, "We will recognize treaty rights. We will recognize forms of contract which have been made with the Indian people by the Crown and we will try to bring justice in that area and this will mean that perhaps the treaties shouldn't go on for-

3. Harold Cardinal, *The Unjust Society*, Edmonton, Alberta: M. G. Hurtiq Ltd., 1969, p. 44.
4. *Ibid.*, p. 140.

ever. It is inconcievable, I think, that in a given society one section of the society have a treaty with the other section of society."

The statement contained several disquieting elements, as viewed within the Indian community. In the first place, it implied that the Indian people were one with the rest of the nation and should not expect special treatment because of historic circumstances. It was obvious to the Indians that they were not on a par with the general society in economic, social, or political terms, and it seemed unlikely that they would achieve parity by abandoning their identity. Historically and culturally they were a separate people, and the only secure future they could see for themselves and their children depended upon their maintaining a separate status within a pluralistic nation. As the Indian chiefs of Alberta phrased it, "Retaining the legal status of Indians is necessary if Indians are to be treated justly. Justice requires that the special history, rights, and circumstances of Indian people be recognized. . . . There is room in Canada for diversity."[5]

Even more disturbing was the suggestion that the treaties were "forms of contract," the terms of which, while enforceable as a matter of law and equity, need not be perpetuated or might even be unilaterally renounced. Such an interpretation of the treaty relationship was not at all in accord with Indian understanding. "However inadequate and highly questionable as treaties are, they are important, for they symbolize the commitment of the Government to our people."[6]

Elsewhere it was observed, "The intent and purpose of the treaties must be our guide, not the precise letter of a foreign language. Treaties that run forever must have room for the

5. "Citizens Plus," a presentation by the Indian Chiefs of Alberta to Right Honorable P. E. Trudeau, Prime Minister, and the Government of Canada, June 1970, pp. 4-5.
6. Cardinal, *The Unjust Society*, p. 43.

changes in the conditions of life. The undertaking of the Government to provide teachers [a proviso in several of the treaties] was a commitment to provide Indian children the educational opportunity equal to their white neighbors. The machinery and livestock symbolized economic development."[7]

And again, "The Indian people see the treaties as the basis of all their rights and status. If the Government expects the cooperation of the Indians in any new policy, it must accept the Indian viewpoint on treaties."

An obvious cause, possibly the major cause, of the deepening dispute between the Indians of Canada and their national government can be traced to the manner in which the Royal Proclamation of 1763 has functioned in policy determination.

In the few instances when questions arising out of the Proclamation have had judicial review, the opinions handed down had a limiting rather than a broadening effect. In one of the leading decisions, for example (*St. Catherine's Milling and Lumber Co. v. the Queen*, 1889), it was held that the tenure of the Indians on lands to which the Proclamation applied was personal and usufructuary, with the real ownership residing in the crown. It was further held that the political sovereignty of the crown of England extended over the lands in question from the date of the Proclamation, thereby terminating the rights of the Indian tribes to govern in their own territories.[8]

This latter view was consistent with an earlier constitutional theory expressed in *Campbell v. Hall* (1774), holding that "a country conquered by British arms becomes a dominion of the King in the right of his Crown and, therefore, necessarily subject to the legislature, the Parliament of Great Britain."[9]

7. "Citizens Plus," p. 8.
8. James A. O'Reilly, "Whither the Indian?" paper prepared for the Civil Liberties Section of the Canadian Bar Association, 1969 annual meeting.
9. Quoted in O'Reilly, *ibid.*, p. 7.

The Canadian tribes, of course, were not conquered by Great Britain but happened to be residing in territory, part of which was taken by force of arms. This judicial theory, nevertheless, was applied to the tribes and was never challenged by them.

What is notable throughout this record, indeed, is the almost total absence of legal challenge by Indian tribes, by officials of government, or citizen groups acting in their behalf. This point is stressed in the study sponsored by the Indian-Eskimo Association of Canada, in which it is observed, "The Indians have been very dependent upon the Federal Government, for Indians have, generally speaking, not gone to court to test or enforce their rights. Unfortunately, this has meant that their legal rights and aboriginal claims are poorly defined in our law. Being poorly defined they could easily be disregarded by the Government when the frame of reference changed, and that has happened."[10]

As a consequence of this historical development, as the report notes, "Half of Canada's Indians entered into treaty at the request of the Crown. The other half were never given that opportunity, in spite of the Royal Proclamation of 1763 and the clear policy of the Federal Government. The claims of half of Canada's Indians were dealt with in an orderly way and on the basis that they had legal possessory rights to surrender. This raises significant questions about the legal correctness of dealing with land in the remaining areas. If a legal remedy exists for non-treaty areas now in non-Indian ownership, it could only be a claim for compensation."[11]

The implication of this last observation would suggest that in the absence of a clear record of court decisions in support of aboriginal entitlement, it is probably impossible for the Indians of Canada to obtain a judgment returning land to tribal owners such as was obtained by the Walapai Indians of Arizona.

10. *Native Rights in Canada*, p. 20.
11. *Ibid.*, p. 204.

This brings sharply to focus the contrasting policies that grew out of the Proclamation of 1763. In both countries, the superior political authority was recognized as inherent in the dominant society; tribal authority became subject to the will of the ruling power.

In the United States, however, the Marshall decisions and later court opinions supported the thesis that tribal sovereignty endured except as, and only to the extent that it was specifically curtailed. Hence, the Indian Reorganization Act of 1934 recognized the right of Indian tribes to adopt written constitutions and to incorporate in such constitutions "all powers vested in any Indian tribe or tribal council by existing law." By enumeration, these "vested powers" covered a wide spectrum of municipal discretion.

In Canada, by contrast, the ruling opinion (*Campbell v. Hall*), as noted, held that the "Indian nations" lost their independent status and became subjects of the king. The Indian Act of Canada is based on this assumption of plenary power, hence the particulate nature of its controls over local initiative.

Another area of contrasting development affected Indian land titles. Again, in both countries the basic doctrine was similar, holding that the legal title was vested in the government, subject to the tribal right of use and occupancy. The lands were inalienable, except that the tribes could convey their interest to the government, or in the event of dissolution of the tribe the legal title became perfected in the sovereign.

A succession of opinions handed down by United States courts defined more clearly and more substantially the nature of tribal right. Thus it has been held that the Indian right of occupancy was "sacred" and could only be extinguished by consent and for acceptable consideration. This right obtained even in the absence of treaty recognition and validation. Tribal reservations were not grants of land from the United States, but were residual estates retained by the tribes out of the larger areas conveyed to the nation. And finally, the tribes, with consent, now formalized by the Indian Claims Commission Act, could always bring legal action to compel the United States to grant redress for wrongful acts.

Canadian law and practice lacked this clarity. The Indian Act defines an Indian reserve as a tract of land set apart by the crown for the use and benefit of an Indian band, which is in keeping with the thesis that the crown holds legal title. What has not been defined is the nature of the "use and benefit" granted by the crown. In the St. Catherine's case it was suggested that Indian rights in the land were not limited to hunting and fishing, but the question has not been further explored.

A recent writer observed, "In effect, if indeed the Indian interest is equivalent to the usufruct of the lands reserved for them . . . it is immediately evident that this right might well extend to the beneficial use of the produce, timber and minerals inherent in or attached to such lands. If one ponders the possibility that the Province cannot by law extinguish this interest, the potential financial benefits which could accrue to the Indians from the recognition of these claims should cause a more responsible reflection and hopefully more enlightened reaction on the part of the Canadian government and most of the provincial governments."[12]

The question was further clouded by a decision of the Supreme Court of Canada in 1969, which held that treaty-protected hunting and fishing rights were invalid against the Migratory Birds Convention, an international agreement. The court in this case acknowledged that the federal government, in adhering to the convention, abrogated the several treaties in which the Indians were guaranteed the right to hunt and fish in the reserved lands as well as in surrounding unoccupied

12. O'Reilly, *op. cit.*, pp. 40-41.

lands. For a people still largely dependent upon a hunting economy, any curtailment of their access to a subsistence base can
only invite tragedy.

Overshadowing even these uncertainties are the unresolved
issues affecting the land promised by treaty but never delivered to the Indians of the Northwest Territory, and the land
rights of the Indians of Yukon Territory and the Eskimo people, with whom no treaties were made. As mineral exploration
and discovery go forward in the north, these questions can only
become more complex and the likelihood of an equitable settlement will diminish as countering interests compete for ful-
fillment.

As early as 1948 an Indian Claims Commission was recommended by a special joint committee of the Canadian Parliament; this commission was to be empowered "to inquire into
the terms of all Indian treaties in order to discover and determine, definitely and finally, such rights and obligations as are
therein involved and . . . settle finally . . . all claims and
grievances which have arisen thereunder."[13]

Attempts to obtain the necessary legislation were made in
1963 and 1965, without success. The idea was revived in 1968
by the Trudeau government and then almost immediately
dropped. In announcing a proposed new Indian policy in June
1969, it was explained, "The Government had intended to in-
troduce legislation to establish an Indian Claims Commission to
hear and determine Indian claims. Consideration of the questions raised at the consultations and review of Indian policy
raised serious doubts as to whether a Claims Commission . . .
is the right way to deal with the grievances of Indians put forward as claims."[14]

13. *Native Rights*, pp. 40-41.
14. *Ibid.*, pp. 192-93.

What was proposed instead was the appointment of a commissioner, whose task would be to classify claims that "in his judgment ought to be referred to the courts or any special quasi-judicial body that may be recommended."

To this it was rejoined, "How can the Indians expect just treatment from a political appointee whose boss is the adversary in any confrontation? The only claims that the commissioner might be expected to submit for adjudication will be those of a token nature that will make the government look good but will not cost too much."

The judgment may have been harsh, but it was the expression of a long experience of being overreached by men in authority.

From what has already been mentioned of the proposed new Indian policy announced in 1969, Indian opposition all across Canada might have been anticipated. The policy statement was based on what the Indian people considered faulty assumptions, and it seemed designed to diminish rather than to enhance their hopes for survival as a native people. The proposal, moreover, bore a striking resemblance to the termination policy of the Eisenhower administration in the United States, whether or not that was the intention.

A careful student of Canadian Indian affairs made this appraisal: "The values of most Canadian Indians are not those of the cultural majority; among other differences, the notion of advancing themselves as individuals rather than members of their group is alien to their culture."

And further, "The vast majority" are those "who still prefer cultural separateness because they have never known anything else, and those who do know something of the white man's world and are willing to undertake the limited experiment of sifting out of their own culture those aspects which they can combine with aspects of the alien culture in such a way as to get on working terms with modern life. . . . They want to remain distinctive; any 'melting pot' process horrifies them; but they are ready for a functional integration, particularly in an economic sense."[15]

Such attitudes, as may be imagined, were not tempered by the stated purpose of the policy declaration: "The Government believes that its policies must lead to the full, free, and non-discriminatory participation of the Indian people in Canadian society. . . . The policies proposed recognize the simple reality that the separate legal status of Indians and the policies that have flowed from it have kept the Indian people apart from and behind other Canadians." And elsewhere, "This Government . . . is determined that all [Canadians] shall be treated fairly and that no one shall be shut out of Canadian life, and especially that no one shall be shut out because of his race."[16]

These statements assumed that the Indian people were prepared to abandon their tribal past and embrace the ways of an alien and often hostile people. They assumed, further, that racial, not cultural barriers, stood in the way of Indian participation in the national economy. The government had only to provide the opportunity, the "framework," in the language of the policy declaration, and the Indians would leap forward.

How far this was from the mark was perhaps best expressed by David Courchene, president of the Manitoba Indian Brotherhood, in a statement submitted to the Indian Affairs Branch of the Canadian government in October 1971. The statement, widely read across Canada, was notably temperate and plain-spoken. It observed, "These last one hundred years have been the time of most difficult struggle, but they have not broken our spirit nor altered our love for this land nor our attachment and commitment to it. We have survived as a people. Our attachment means that we must also commit ourselves to help

15. John Melling, "A Survey of the Present Situation of Indians in Canada," *Indian Truth*, vol. 47, no. 1, Feb. 1970, pp. 1-12.
16. "Statement of the Government of Canada on Indian Policy," Minister of Indian Affairs and Northern Development, Ottawa, 1969.

develop healthy societies for all the people who live upon this land. But we will not be able to contribute unless we have the means first to develop a healthy society for ourselves. Since the signing of the treaties one hundred years ago, we have been constantly and consistently prevented from doing so."[17]

In two specific areas, the proposed policy misinterpreted the sentiments of the Indian people. It was suggested, for example, that the six million acres of land held in trust by the Canadian government should eventually be transferred to the Indians in full title and made subject to taxation. The wording was explicit: "The Government believes that full ownership implies many things. It carries with it the free choice of use, of retention or of disposition. In our society it also carries with it an obligation to pay for certain services. . . . When the Indian people see that the only way they can own and fully control land is to accept taxation the way other Canadians do, they will make that decision."[18]

This echoed an old grievance—the white man's insistence that his attitude toward land was the only proper attitude and that Indians must reform their practices. An Indian critic observed, "The idea that a human being should say that this piece of land or water or sky belongs to him has traditionally been a concept foreign to the Indian. . . . When the Indians signed treaties with the Crown, they gave up certain portions of land that they had used before. They viewed the reserved lands as lands that they kept not only for themselves but for the generations to follow them. . . . They do not feel they have the right to decide on the status of their reserves unless they are able to consult with generations yet to be born."[19]

The Indians wanted control of their lands, as they wanted

17. David Courchene, "Wahbung, Our Tomorrow," quoted in *The Montreal Star*, Oct. 16, 1971.
18. "Statement . . . on Indian Policy," p. 12.
19. Cardinal, *The Unjust Society*, p. 158.

control over other areas of their social and economic interests, but they were not prepared to abandon traditional values and transform their land holdings into taxable and merchantable pieces of impersonal real estate. They saw no inconsistency in wanting control and at the same time maintaining the inalienability of the lands protected by treaty guarantees.

The other area of misunderstanding worth noting had to do with the relationship of Indians with the several provinces. The policy statement declared, "Canadians receive a wide range of services through provincial and local governments, but the Indian people and their communities are mostly outside that framework. It is no longer acceptable that the Indian people should be outside and apart. . . . Services ought not to flow from separate agencies established to serve particular groups, especially not to groups that are defined ethnically."[20]

The Indians found these declarations unsettling, however altruistic the intention might have been. It seemed to Indian spokesmen that the federal government was trying to relieve itself of further responsibility by shifting the burden and expense of Indian affairs management to the provinces. They contended that the mere shifting of responsibility would not solve for the Indian people the problems they shared as a consequence of their economic disabilities, their low level of educational opportunity, their exceptional health problems, and the lack of an adequate resource base. Even with federal assistance, as proposed by the policy statement, it seemed questionable to them whether the provinces could or would maintain adequate services. A spokesman remarked, "We have no treaties with provincial governments, but we do with the Federal Government, even if they are not honored."

After more than a century of comparative silence, as decisions affecting their lives and their property were made by cabinet ministers, courts, civil servants, and others, the Indians

20. "Statement . . . on Indian Policy," p. 9.

of Canada were insisting that their voices be heard. Strong leadership emerged all across the country, even in the remote north, as the national government was forced to recognize, a consequence of which was the modification of much of the position taken by the Trudeau government in 1969.

Thus, while they had no head of government to speak for tribal self-determination, the Indians of Canada in the 1970s were discovering, as were their kinsmen elsewhere in North America, that self-determination was an instrument which only they could fit to their hands. Others might proclaim it as a philosophy of human interaction, but the people involved must learn how to make it work.

9 EPILOGUE IN ALASKA

The Treaty of Cession by which Alaska passed from Russia to the United States in 1867 assured the "liberty, property, and religion" of those Russian subjects who chose to remain in Alaska, an assurance that extended to many settled natives, principally Aleuts. Natives not living in Russian settlements, referred to in the treaty as "the uncivilized tribes," were to be "subject to such laws and regulations as the United States may, from time to time, adopt in regard to the aboriginal tribes of that country."

The lack of precision in this wording had the unfortunate effect of casting a cloud over the rights of the Natives in the land they had occupied for at least four thousand years. It rendered them subject to the laws of a foreign government without clearly specifying what obligation that government assumed in their behalf.

The United States adopted some corrective measures in later years, without, however, removing the ambiguity. Thus, as already mentioned in Chapter 3, the Act of 1884 establishing civil government in the territory provided "that the Indians or other persons in said district shall not be disturbed in the possession of any lands actually in their use or occupation or now claimed by them." The wording here seemed to place Indians and "other persons" on the same footing as land owners, with no indication that Natives might have prior rights by reason of aboriginal occupancy, or that "others" might be in possession of lands to which the aboriginal title had not been previously extinguished. Both classes of owners, Indians and "other," moreover, could not be certain of their status on the land since the act further provided that "the terms under which such persons may acquire title to such lands is reserved for future legislation by Congress."

A later enactment was somewhat more specific in protecting the Native in his own country. That was the 1891 act extending to Alaska the Homestead Act which allowed individuals to acquire 160 acres of public land, but expressly exempted "any lands . . . to which the Natives of Alaska have prior rights by virtue of actual occupation."

In still other instances, provision was made for reserving waterfront sites as landing places for Native canoes or other craft, and for 160-acre home sites, title to which would be inalienable and non-taxable, until Congress determined otherwise.

Besides these modest concessions to the original inhabitants, small reserves were set aside for school purposes, usually not more than forty acres, and somewhat larger areas were designated as reindeer reserves after those animals were introduced as herd animals toward the end of the last century. Very few Natives took advantage of the provision allowing for home site locations, and the effect of these early policies was negligible in resolving the land question.

These several enactments followed no set policy but were expedient and piecemeal attempts to deal with a major problem of Indian-white relations in a frontier society. The situation continued until 1936, when Congress made the first serious effort to fulfill the promise of 1884 to set the terms by which Natives might acquire title to the lands they occupied.

The instrument was the 1936 Alaska Amendment to the Indian Reorganization Act of 1934, which empowered the Secretary of the Interior to designate as an Indian reservation any area of land used and occupied by Indians or Eskimos, together with adjacent areas of public lands, as the Secretary might determine to be feasible. The designation by the Secretary was not effective, however, until the Indians or Eskimos voted by secret ballot to accept the reservation. The latter provision was intended to allow an opportunity for a native group to participate in the selection of the land and to reject what might be deemed inadequate or unacceptable, for whatever reason.

The legislation did not accomplish what was expected of it, partly because its purposes were not understood and partly because those purposes were obscured in partisan debate. Only six reservations were accepted by native electorates, while in three other instances the Secretary's designation was rejected.

The apparent reluctance of the Native communities to request reserves of land under the authority of the 1936 legislation was a reflection of their distrust of government policy. They had been left relatively undisturbed in their daily pursuits, even in the absence of legal determination of their rights, and they feared that accepting a reservation might limit their freedom to move about. Native children transported by the government to distant boarding schools at Chemawa in Oregon and Carlisle in Pennsylvania learned to resent the heavy-handed school officials, and their contacts with Indians in the States only intensified their distrust of the white man in authority. Later, as adults, they spoke out against placing themselves under government supervision.[1]

1. A brief history of this period is contained in the "Report to the Secretary of the Interior by the Task Force on Alaskan Native Affairs," Washington, D.C., 1962.

These uncertainties and fears were freely played upon by individuals and corporate entities, whose interests were often in direct conflict with the claims of native communities. In these quarters, the idea of aboriginal rights in the land was bitterly opposed. Mining men, commercial fisheries, and chambers of commerce in such cities as Juneau and Ketchikan insisted that Congress adopt legislation extinguishing all Indian land titles, excepting only small home sites, and allowing the Natives redress through court proceedings. To one such proposal, offered in 1949 by the Juneau chamber of commerce, the Secretary of the Interior replied, "The solution which your draft bill proposes is in some respects a tempting one, in that it would forthwith eliminate all Native claims to the public domain in Alaska, without the necessity of a tedious inquiry into what may in fact be their land rights. I do not, however, consider that such an approach is consistent with our national traditions. Our government has always respected property rights, of persons of all races."[2]

Commercial interests were especially disturbed by one of the reservations established in accordance with the 1936 Alaska Amendment. The reservation contained 1.4 million acres located on the north slope of the Brooks Range, at the top of the Arctic Plain, an area thinly inhabited by Eskimo hunters and fishermen. The criticism took no account of the nature of the terrain and the precarious ecological balance it sustained, but centered entirely on surface area. It was charged that the Secretary, unless prevented, would give Alaska away to the Natives and legislation was introduced to curtail the Secretary's power to create reservations. At hearings on that legislation in 1948, Senator Butler of Nebraska was explicit in stating the view of private enterprise: "Those of us who are interested in getting

2. Hearings on S.2037 and S.J.Res.162, 80th Congress, 2nd session, Feb.-March 1948.

Alaska developed are anxious that the opportunity be thrown open to all Americans alike, regardless of reservations or Natives located there. We want them to have all their full rights, just like other Americans, but we don't want the rights of the Americans denied at the same time that we are protecting the rights of this small group."[3]

These unforeseen hazards—the distrust of the Natives and the opposition of private business—defeated the efforts of the Roosevelt administration to bring to realization the government's long standing pledge to confirm Native land titles. There were some compensating gains, however. The credit program authorized by the Indian Reorganization Act, when extended to Alaska, resulted in substantial improvement in the economy. Fish canneries and fish traps were constructed at some villages, and when fish traps were outlawed throughout the territory, Native fishermen were able to invest in seine boats. A chain of consumer cooperatives and arts-and-crafts marketing cooperatives was established. Village government was strengthened by defining and formalizing its scope. Education and health facilities were greatly expanded.

These were notable achievements, but in spite of the enlarged government effort the condition of Native life deteriorated as the result of increased competition for the fisheries, the trapping grounds, and the wild game upon which the people depended. An Assistant Secretary of the Interior, testifying before the Senate in 1948, remarked, "As regards Native economic needs, the Native population of Alaska is, on the whole, in a deplorable economic position. Its tuberculosis rate is about ten times as high as the normal rate. This is primarily the result of inadequate food and inadequate, overcrowded housing. . . . In order to enjoy a year round economy and to improve their own housing, the Natives need sawmills, power plants, canneries,

3. *Ibid.,* p. 29

and machine shops. They cannot invest money or attract capital for such development unless their titles are clearly established."[4]

When statehood for the territory was proposed after World War II, the Natives were understandably apprehensive. They wanted their rights determined in advance of statehood, thus avoiding possible conflicts of interest between their claims and the demands of the new state. Legislation was introduced in 1953 purporting "to settle possessory land claims in Alaska," but it failed in a Congress preoccupied with terminating federal responsibility for Indian affairs.

The 1958 legislation authorizing statehood should have quieted Native doubts. It stipulated, "As a compact with the United States, said State and its people do agree and declare that they forever disclaim all right and title . . . to any lands or other property (including fishing rights), the right or title to which may be held by any Indians, Eskimos, or Aleuts." The same disclaimer, in identical language, was then incorporated into the constitution of the new state—a condition that had been accepted by other states as the nation extended westward into Indian country. However, the problem was left where it had always been—in Congress. Their possessory rights were not denied, as the Natives feared might happen, but neither were they defined and measured out in metes and bounds. The situation created by the Treaty of Cession remained unchanged.

The issue finally came to a head when the state, acting in accordance with the enabling legislation, began to make the selections of land to which the legislation entitled it. Almost immediately the selections encroached upon or encompassed areas used and occupied by the inhabitants of native villages.

Regional organizations of Natives quickly came into existence, replacing the older Alaska Native Brotherhood and Alaska Native Sisterhood, which had functioned almost exclusively among the more acculturated villages in southeastern Alaska. The new

4 *Ibid.*, p. 29.

organizations, which spread rapidly across Alaska, westward to the Aleutian Islands, and eastward along the Arctic coast and into the interior, were initially concerned with protecting lands in traditional use. Then in 1966 the Alaska Federation of Natives, representing the constituent villages, was organized to provide a common political force. One of the first accomplishments of the federation was to persuade the Secretary of the Interior, as administrator of public lands, to halt all state selections until the Natives could be secured in the lands claimed by them. The state protested this drastic step, which had the effect of halting its economic development, but the Natives prevailed. Ironically, Walter J. Hickel, who was governor of Alaska at the time and who attempted court action to force the Secretary of the Interior to lift his injunction, later became Secretary and found himself enforcing the order. The effect of this joint effort of Indians, Eskimos, and Aleuts—the first time in their history that they made common cause—was greatly to influence political alignments in the new state. Taken together, the Natives constituted about 30 per cent of the total population, a sufficient force to inspire respect.

The land freeze and the pressures resulting from it were persuasive in bringing about a resolution. The initial step was taken at Anchorage, Alaska, in October 1966 when some 300 representatives of native villages met to draft legislation. From then until passage of the Act of Settlement in December 1971, a number of proposals were considered. The discovery of extensive petroleum deposits on the Arctic slope not only hastened the legislative process but resulted in a more favorable settlement than might otherwise have been possible.

The Department of the Interior, for example, proposed in 1967 that not more than 10 million acres of land be reserved, while allowing the Natives to sue in the United States Court of Claims for the money value of any lands in excess of that amount, should the court find them entitled to a larger area.

The proposal was completely unacceptable to the Native leaders, who held that their title to 90 per cent of Alaska's land area, or about 340 million acres, had never been extinguished. In their first countering proposal, the leaders indicated a willingness to settle for sixty million acres, or approximately 17 per cent of the total area claimed. They also asked for $500 million as partial compensation for the relinquished area and a 2 per cent revenue tax on oil and minerals extracted from the relinquished lands.

While these preliminary negotiations were in process, Alaska received $900 million from a consortium of oil companies interested in exploring for oil on the Arctic slope. The payment of such a sum in September 1969 made the asking price of the Native leaders seem almost modest.

The Settlement Act as finally worked out between the two houses of Congress contained the basic terms originally proposed by the Natives. In a special message to Congress in April 1971, the President expressed support for the legislation: "The new bill, . . . developed in close consultation with representatives of the Alaska Federation themselves, provides for a cash payment of $500 million and also provides that the Natives shall have a two per cent share, up to a maximum of $500 million, in the oil revenues generated in Alaska; that they shall have full title to 40 million acres of land, and that the corporation that manages these assets shall be entirely Native controlled."[5]

On December 14, 1971, action was completed in Congress and the Settlement Act went to the President for signature.

After more than four hundred years, a native people and a colonizing power had come to terms. What had been expressed as a piety by Spanish humanists, then elevated into law in British North America, had met the harsh test of the market. The Natives of Alaska had asserted their rights as original owners of the soil—rights which priests, statesmen, and jurists had recog-

5. White House press release, April 6, 1971.

nized, and frontier society had largely ignored—and their claim had been honored. While it can be argued that victory for the Natives was achieved for the wrong reason—the desire to gain access to Alaska's riches even at the cost of recognizing and paying for aboriginal rights of occupancy—it must also be acknowledged that the settlement could have ignored the prior rights of the native people. It would have been wholly in the tradition of Western colonialism to have taken the land on a presumption of superior usage, as indeed it was argued in the United States Senate. In this case, for once, necessity was the mother of virtue.

At the very least, it can be asserted that the settlement, on terms approximating the views put forth by the Alaska Natives, established a useful precedent. It should be more difficult in future for a dominant industrial power to act without regard for underlying human rights.

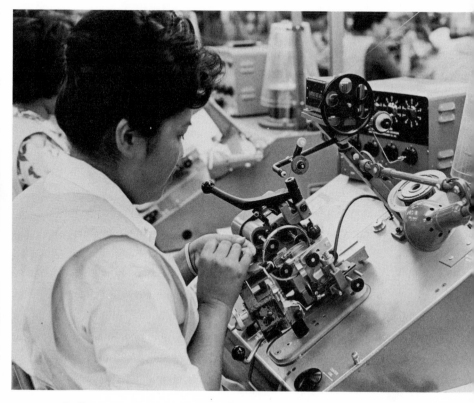

Indian operators working in electronics plant owned by Laguna Pueblo, New Mexico.

Theodore B. Hetzel

Assembling electronics devices, Laguna Pueblo.

Theodore B. Hetzel

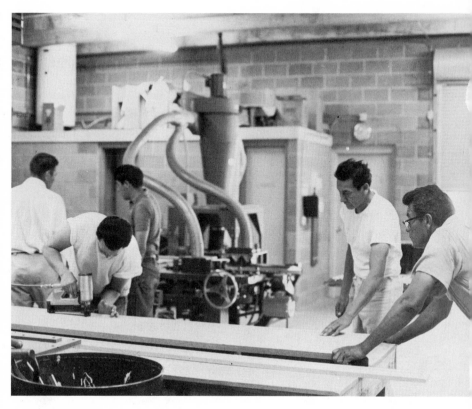

Making laminated plastic kitchen cabinets, Rosebud Reservation, South Dakota.

Theodore B. Hetzel

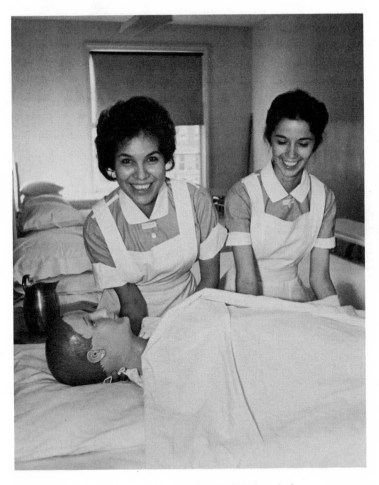

Indian girls training as nurses in a Philadelphia hospital.

Theodore B. Hetzel

Prize-winning sheep, Zuni Pueblo, New Mexico.

Theodore B. Hetzel

Cattle raising on the Pine Ridge Reservation, South Dakota, one of the major Sioux tribes.

Theodore B. Hetzel

10 A CLOSING VIEW

After these many years of inter-ethnic contact in the New World, it is not yet possible to say that the relationship between white man and Indian is free of the presumptuous bias that marked its beginnings. Indians may no longer be expected to vanish before a competition "they had not the means of sustaining," but their moral right to remain a separate and identifiable people is far from assured.

The safeguards against oppression founded in the humanistic traditions of the Western world were time and again ignored or denied by the dynamics of conquest. Pope Alexander enjoined peaceful conversion, but the Spanish invaders in establishing New World dominion slaughtered and enslaved as suited their purposes. The crown of England declared a boundary separating Indian country from the settled areas of colonial North America but could not contain the energies that drove men westward in quest of wealth and power.

The pattern of affirmation and denial established in the first years of contact has never been outlived or outmoded. Men in the dominant society who labored to defend the interests of tribal people were invariably matched by men who resented the existence of "savages," particularly if they controlled landed property and presumed to autonomy in the conduct of their affairs. A John Marshall, speaking out for the right of an Indian tribe to exercise jurisdiction over its native homeland, was matched by an Andrew Jackson who swept the tribes out of the southeast rather than defend their right to determine where and how they wished to live. Bringing the antithetical pattern down to modern times, the effort of the John Collier administration to restore tribal primacy in internal rule was all but destroyed by the negativism of the United States Senate in the Eisenhower years.

For the Indians of Canada, so little of what they once owned was confirmed to them and so much denied as to leave their future in precarious balance. Only recently have they been aroused to the peril in which they live as tribal people.

It remains to be determined whether in North America self-determination for an indigenous people is to have ideological acceptance and thereby attain enduring political sanction. Certain events discussed in this brief historical review, and some not yet mentioned, would seem to favor an emerging policy of sanctioned self-determination.

One of these is the confirmation of aboriginal land titles in Alaska. While the settlement was achieved in response to the urgings of industrial conglomerates wholly indifferent to and possibly inimical to native interests, as noted above, nevertheless the Natives have assurance that they may now pursue their accustomed lives in communities of their own making. Change will come to those communities, but choice can be exercised as to what changes are accepted.

An event not previously mentioned should be noted here, since it adds another dimension to the range of ethnic policy.

This has to do with the long struggle of the Taos Indians of New Mexico to reclaim their Blue Lake shrine.

Long before the Spaniards came to New Mexico, the Taos people had looked to the neighboring mountains for spiritual experience, formalized in ceremonial practices. In particular, they journeyed each year to mystic Blue Lake nestled high in a bowl on a 12,000-foot mountain, where their young adults were initiated and assumed their roles as functioning members of the community. The ceremonies were held secretly, far from the prying eyes of the curious.

In 1906, the Taos mountain and connecting watershed on which the village depended for its water supply were incorporated into an adjoining national forest. Very soon afterward the Indians discovered that they could not use the forest or forest products without first obtaining permission from an indifferent bureaucracy; moreover, permits to graze livestock or to take timber were awarded to outsiders, and the Indians found themselves intruded upon when they went to the mountain for ceremonial purposes.

Their first efforts to secure the return of their sacred mountain were given scant attention. This was at a time when the view still prevailed that the Indian people would vanish and ranking government officials deemed it of small consequence that an obscure tribe complained of interference with its pagan practices.

In later years, when the Indians did not disappear and concerned citizens involved themselves in the affair, the government maintained that perpetuation of the forest required that it be managed by scientifically trained supervisors, in face of the fact that the Taos Indians had kept the forest in an unblemished state since before the white man entered the region. The question of ownership of the mountain and surrounding territory was submitted to the Indian Claims Commission, and this resulted in a finding in favor of the Taos Pueblo with compensation to be determined as of the time of taking. The Pueblo, however, rejected a money award and insisted on the return of the land.

In December 1971, after sixty-five years of unremitting effort by the Pueblo, Congress capitulated and adopted legislation restoring the land to its rightful owners. Of interest here, is that the Pueblo all along had based its plea for return of the land on religious grounds, not on the economic value of the real estate. Such a plea was regarded with contempt when first offered, and the fact that finally it was accepted as valid is a measure of the distance traveled toward a policy of cultural tolerance, which must be the basis of any commitment in support of self-determination.

Moreover, the Taos incident did not occur in isolation. Encouraged by that example, the Yakima Indians in the State of Washington and the Warm Springs Indians in Oregon petitioned for and obtained the return of lands wrongfully taken from them. These latter transactions were the first in which land was restored to Indian claimants without prolonged and costly legislative or court battles. They reflected a profound change of attitude toward the Indian people and their rights vis-à-vis the dominant society.

All through North America, from the Arctic to the Florida peninsula, the long submerged Indian minority has been discovering the value of the published word, and this may prove to be the decisive force in bringing into being an enduring policy of self-determined cultural pluralism. Surveying publications at the beginning of the 1970s, the Smithsonian Institution reported more than a hundred items currently published by Indian and Indian interest organizations. Some of these dealt only with local news, but others carried information and critical articles dealing with national issues. One such publication, *Akwesasne Notes*, carried news stories and editorial comment from all over North America, Mexico, and South America. Its outspoken editorial policy quickly established it as a major voice in telling the Indian point of view in causes at issue.

Indian expression was not limited to social protest. The Kiowa-Pueblo novelist, N. Scott Momaday, won the Pulitzer Prize for fiction in 1969. Indian poets and songwriters are appearing in print. Indian painters, who had to overcome the stereotype of two-dimensional, non-perspective compositions which won them early praise from a patronizing public, now move boldly into the art market. The themes are traditional, but the execution is personal and evocative. In the professions, in social science especially, Indian scholars bring fresh insight in discourses on the condition of man in the modern world.

In all of this, the orientation is notably tribal and traditional, either newly discovered or reaffirmed. The Indian political voice as well as their creative expression reject the values of the dominant society and turn inward for individual and group support. Indian nationalism, pan-Indianism, Red Power—terms used with some degree of common meaning—indicate a growing sense of shared problems, shared goals, and a shared heritage. Such terms are likely to be rejected outright by the older generation, but it should not be inferred from this that the old and the young are at odds; it means only that the grandfathers are not at ease with new English words. However, while words may confuse the elders, they are not confused about who they are. It is this certainty of self which the young proclaim, sometimes loudly. There is no such certainty for them in the white man's affluent society.

Finally, it can be noted in closing that the spokesmen of earlier years who tried to accept what an alien world offered their people, seeing no other choice open, are now silent. If the Indian race is to be destroyed, the new voices avow, the destroying agent will have to contend with an integrating tribal people, not with isolated individuals lost in anonymity.

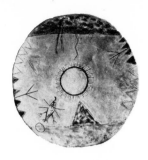

APPENDIX

Geographical Distribution
of the Principal Tribes: United States

Southwest

The region consists of the states of New Mexico and Arizona. It contains the greatest number of culturally and biologically distinct Indians.

The dominant group in the Southwest region is the Navajo tribe, numbering 122,316 in 1969. It is also one of the fastest growing tribal populations, having increased at least tenfold within a hundred years. The Navajos and their linguistic kinsmen, the Apaches, of the Athapascan stock, are late arrivals in the Southwest.

The Navajo reservation of some 25,000 square miles extends over parts of New Mexico, Arizona, and Utah.

The Apaches, with a population in excess of 14,000, are located on four reserved areas, Jicarilla and Mescalero in New Mexico, and Fort Apache and San Carlos in Arizona.

Along the southern border of Arizona are found the Pimanspeaking Pima and Papago tribes, each on separate reservations, with a combined population of 16,340.

Westward along the lower Colorado River are several small tribes of the Yuman linguistic stock: Havasupai, Walapai, Yavapai, Mohave, Yuma, and Cocopa, with a population all told of 5343. A linguistically related group, the Maricopas, are found with the Pima tribe near Phoenix, Arizona.

The so-called Pueblo tribes, representing several linguistic groups, are distributed principally along the Rio Grande River in New Mexico, but a few are found in western New Mexico and northern Arizona. They are village dwelling Indians, as the Spanish term signifies.

New Mexico Pueblos	Language		Population
Cochiti	Keresan		700
San Felipe	"		1340
Santa Ana	"		422
Santo Domingo	"		2058
Sia	"		479
Jemez	Tanoan (Jemez)		1528
Nambe	" (Tewa)		237
Pojoaque	"	"	60
San Ildefonso	"	"	319
San Juan	"	"	1255
Santa Clara	"	"	916
Tesuque	"	"	231
Isleta	" (Tiwa)		2356
Picuris	"	"	165
Sandia	"	"	211
Taos	"	"	1470
Western Pueblos			
Acoma	Keresan		2512
Laguna	"		4432
Zuni	Zuni		5352
Hopi	Shoshonean		6000
		TOTAL	32,043

Basin and Plateau

This intermontane region, stretching from the southern boundary of Utah northward through Idaho and western Montana, is inhabited by a number of small tribes. The region is generally high and arid, a country of wide shallow basins contained within heavily eroded mountain ranges. In the north, rainfall increases and scrub and sage brush gives way to pine forests, and perennial streams abound.

In the southern portion—southern Colorado, Utah, and Nevada—the numerous small tribes and camps belong almost entirely to the Shoshonean division of the Uto-Aztecan linguistic stock. The principal of these are as follows:

State	Tribe	Population
Colorado	Ute (two bands)	1917
Utah	Ute	1640
Nevada	Paiute	3412
	Goshute	200
	Shoshone	2100
	Washo (Hokan)	1200
	TOTAL	10,469

The tribes in the northern portion of the region are settled on larger reservations, hence there is less scattering of the Indian population. Several linguistic stocks are represented.

State	Tribe	Population
Idaho	Bannock (Shoshonean)	600
	Coeur d'Alene (Salishan)	511
	Kalispel (Salishan)	102
	Kutenai (Algonquian-Wakashan)	67
	Nez Perce (Shapwailutan)	2251
	Shoshone (Uto-Aztecan)	2440
Montana	Salish-Kutenai (Salishan)	5300

Oregon (Eastern)	Klamath (Penutian)	2133
	Paiute (Shoshonean)	350
	Umatilla (Shapwailutan)	1245
	Warm Springs	
	(Chinookan)	1761
Washington (Eastern)	Colville (Salishan)	4952
	Kalispel "	167
	Spokane "	1500
	Yakima (Shapwailutan)	5391

California

The California-Oregon coastal area is a region of great linguistic complexity with approximately one-third of all the languages spoken north of Mexico found in the area. The tribes and bands were often quite small in numbers and the territory occupied limited in area.

The contemporary situation is still one of great complexity, though the tribes have dwindled to even smaller dimensions, and most of the land base has been fraudulently seized. The California region was the most heavily populated of all native regions in pre-discovery times, and proportionately it suffered the greatest losses through epidemics, loss of economic base, and slaughter, which reached a peak immediately after the discovery of gold. The Indian population of the state was estimated at 100,000 in 1853; it dropped to 48,000 in 1856; to 30,000 in 1864, and 19,014 in 1906. This represented a loss of 81 per cent in a period of fifty years. The population in 1960 was given as 39,014.

The principal extant tribes are as follows:

Tribe	Linguistic affiliation	Population
Achomawi	Hokan-Siouan	328
Diegueno (26 settlements)	Yuman	7693

Hupa	Athapascan	1271
Karok	Hokan-Siouan	120
Luiseno	Shoshonean	888
Maidu	Penutian	178
Miwok	"	130
Paiute-Shoshone	Shoshonean	2276
Pomo	Hokan-Siouan	916
Wintun	Penutian	179
Yokuts	"	504
Yurok	Algonquian	959

Northwest Coast

The nurturing center of the Northwest Coast culture was probably along the Fraser River in British Columbia and adjacent Vancouver Island, whence it spread southward to the Indians of Oregon and northern California, up the Columbia and other coast rivers, but attaining its greatest richness in what is now southeastern Alaska.

The tribes of the region are numerous, often small in population, and quite a few have lost their identity by merging with other tribes or have become extinct. The larger of the extant tribes are as follows:

Tribe	State	Linguistic affiliation	Population
Chastacosta	Oregon	Athapascan	30
Chehalis	Washington	Salishan (Coastal)	186
Clackamas	Oregon	Chinookan	89
Clallam	Washington	Salishan (Coastal)	1205
Lummi	"	"	1200
Makah	"	Wakashan	558
Muckleshoot	"	Salishan (Coastal)	340
Nisqually	"	"	189
Nooksack	"	"	303
Puyallup	"	"	479

Quileute	Washington	Chimakuan (Wakashan)	270
Quinault	”	Salishan (Coastal)	1050
Skagit	”	”	259
Skokomish	”	”	230
Snohomish	”	”	994
Suquamish	”	”	181
Swinomish	”	”	364
Tututni	Oregon	Athapascan	110
Umpqua	”	”	149

The Great Plains

The Indians of the Plains region, perhaps more than any other, typify the North American Indian in stereotype. He is the Indian of the eagle feather headdress, the buffalo hunt, the skin tipi, the nomadic horseman. He was the last to be encountered and brushed aside as the course of settlement moved across the frontier, and for that reason he is still vivid in the national consciousness. It can be said, indeed, that the Plains Indian was a product of the conquest of the Americas, for it was the bringing of the horse to the New World that made him the archetype of the red Indian.

The principal tribes of the Great Plains are as follows:

Tribe	State	Linguistic affiliation	Population
Arapaho	Wyoming	Algonquian	2102
Arikara	North Dakota	Caddoan	1408
Assiniboin	Montana	Siouan	3424
Atsina (Gros Ventre)	”	Algonquian	2133
Blackfoot	”	”	10,467
Cheyenne	”	”	2906
Cheyenne-Arapaho	Oklahoma	(Not enumerated separately)	3700
Comanche	”	Shoshonean	2694

Cree	Montana	Algonquian	1486
Crow	"	Siouan	4828
Dakota	Minnesota	"	1133
"	Montana	"	3000
"	Nebraska	"	1372
"	North Dakota	"	8760
"	South Dakota	"	37,380
Hidatsa (Gros Ventre)	North Dakota	"	1558
Kiowa	Oklahoma	Kiowa-Tanoan	2692
Mandan	North Dakota	Siouan	705
Osage	Oklahoma	"	4923
Pawnee	"	Caddoan	1149
Ponca	"	Siouan	926

Eastern Region

Relatively few of the tribes which had their homelands east of the Mississippi River remain *in situ*. The Indian Removal Act of 1830 authorized the President to negotiate agreements with the eastern Indians, by the terms of which the Indians were moved out of the settled areas into a region west of the Mississippi vaguely defined as Indian Territory. Many such displaced tribes are today found in Oklahoma.

The principal remaining tribes are as follows:

Tribe	State	Linguistic affiliation	Population
Alabama-Coushatta	Texas	Muskoghean	550
Caddo	Oklahoma	Caddoan	1184
Cayuga	New York	Iroquoian	233
Cherokee	North Carolina	"	4266
"	Oklahoma	"	25,600
Chickasaw	"	Muskoghean	3600
Chitimacha	Louisiana	Tunican	600
Chippewa	Michigan	Algonquian	2049
"	Minnesota	"	27,318

"	North Dakota	"	11,311
"	Wisconsin	"	5308
Choctaw	Mississippi	Muskoghean	3185
"	Oklahoma	"	16,000
Creek	"	"	16,640
Delaware	"	Algonquian	1385
Kickapoo	Kansas	"	426
"	Oklahoma	"	283
Menominee	Wisconsin	"	3570
Miami	Oklahoma	"	323
Mohawk	New York	Iroquoian	2222
Oneida	New York	Iroquoian	526
"	Wisconsin	"	5184
Onondaga	New York	"	1068
Ottawa	Oklahoma	Algonquian	488
Peoria	"	"	414
Potawatomi	Kansas	"	2128
"	Michigan	"	200
"	Oklahoma	"	2976
"	Wisconsin	"	229
Sauk and Fox	Iowa	"	795
"	Kansas	"	250
"	Oklahoma	"	996
Seminole	Florida	Muskoghean	1186
"	Oklahoma	"	2900
Seneca	New York	Iroquoian	5403
"	Oklahoma	"	930
Shawnee	"	Algonquian	1442
Stockbridge-Munsee	Wisconsin	Mahican-Munsee	920
Tuscarora	New York	Iroquoian	650
Wichita	Oklahoma	Caddoan	460
Winnebago	Nebraska	Siouan	1813
"	Wisconsin	"	1330
Wyandotte	Oklahoma	Iroquoian	894

Alaska

The Indians, Eskimos, and Aleuts of Alaska are village dwellers scattered along the extensive coastline and along the waterways of the interior. Since theirs was basically a hunting economy adapted to the sea or to the uplands, concentrations of population were exceptional, occurring only in the southeastern panhandle. Language distribution, by contrast, is characterized by the extensive spread of linguistic homogeneity. Eskimo-speakers, for example, occupy some 6000 miles of coastline from the Gulf of Alaska and across the Arctic all the way to Greenland. The Athapaskan cognate languages are found throughout the vast interior of Alaska and eastward across northern Canada.

The language groups are distributed as follows:

Region	Language group	Population
Southeast	Tlingit (Nadene)	6063
"	Haida "	842
"	Tsimshian (Penutian)	860
Aleutian Archipelago	Aleut (2 languages)	2416
Bering Sea-Artic Coast	Eskimo (2 languages)	32,846
Interior	Athapaskan (Nadene)	8511

Canada

The Indians and Eskimos of Canada are widely scattered throughout the provinces and territories in numerous small reserves that bear but little resemblance to the extensive territories which once subsisted them. Not all of Canada's indigenous people are located on reserved lands, however, since treaties either were not negotiated or, as in the Northwest Territories, were not consummated. Most of the aboriginal population is affiliated with some four major linguistic groups, and the entire population is embraced within eleven groups, including the Eskimoan.

Within each linguistic group is found a varying number of cognate languages, as follows:

Linguistic Group	Associated Languages	Population
Algonquian	Abenaki	616
	Algonquin	4514
	Blackfoot	7310
	Cree	60,597
	Delaware	581
	Malecite	1626
	Micmac	8645
	Montagnais	5268
	Naskapi	284
	Ojibwa	43,948
	Ottawa	1495
	Potawatomi	833
Wakashan	Haisla	768
	Heiltsuk	1198
	Kwakiutl	2593
	Nootka	3135
Salishan	Bella Coola	575
	Comox	783
	Cowichan	5652
	Lilooet	2374
	Ntlakyapamuk	2647
	Okanagan	1503
	Puntlatch	41
	Seechelt	447
	Semiahmoo	282
	Shuswap	3675
	Songish	1040
	Squamish	1167
Kootenayan	Kutenai	549
Athapaskan	Beaver	727
	Carrier	3862
	Chilcotin	1594
	Chipewyan	4643
	Dogrib	1068
	Hare	679

	Kutchin	1138
	Loucheux	1112
	Nahani	950
	Sarcee	404
	Sekani	425
	Slave	3004
	Tahltan	656
	Yellowknife	466
Haida	Haida	1315
Tlingit	Tagish	582
Iroquoian	Huron	969
	Iroquois	20,342
Hokan-Siouan	Assiniboine	3110
	Sioux	2503
Penutian (Tsimshian)	Gitsan	2313
	Niska	2145
	Tsimshian	2706
Eskimoan	Eskimo	11,000

Sources:
United States Department of Interior, Bureau of Indian Affairs, *Indian Population,* 1970 Census, Washington, D.C., 1971.
United States Department of Commerce, Economic Development Administration, *Federal and State Reservations,* Washington, D. C., 1971.
Department of Indian Affairs and Northern Development, *Linguistic and Cultural Affiliations of Canadian Indian Bands,* Ottawa, 1967.

INDEX